PAUL
THE APOSTLE OF GRACE
THE MAN TO WHOM CHRIST
GAVE THE FINAL GOSPEL

WARREN LITZMAN

Visit Christ-life Fellowship at www.christ-life.org.

Paul, The Apostle of Grace

Scripture quotations are from
The King James Version of the Holy Bible.

Cover illustration and interior illustrations by
James (Jim) E. Seward, used with permission,
with fond memories and much gratitude.

Christ-life Publishing House
Dallas, Texas
United States of America

ISBN-10: 0-9916140-3-8
ISBN-13: 978-0-9916140-3-5

TABLE OF CONTENTS

FORWARD   v

PREFACE   1

CHAPTER 1   **Paul and the Gentiles**   21
                 CHAPTER 1 REVIEW QUESTIONS   32

CHAPTER 2   **Paul and the Cross**   35
                 CHAPTER 2 REVIEW QUESTIONS   46

CHAPTER 3   **Paul and the Holy Spirit**   49
                 CHAPTER 3 REVIEW QUESTIONS   68

CHAPTER 4   **Paul and the C & S Gang**   71
                 CHAPTER 4 REVIEW QUESTIONS   85

CHAPTER 5   **Paul and the Law**   89
                 CHAPTER 5 REVIEW QUESTIONS   107

CHAPTER 6   **Paul and the Mind**   111
                 CHAPTER 6 REVIEW QUESTIONS   136

CHAPTER 7   **Paul and Religion**   139
                 CHAPTER 7 REVIEW QUESTIONS   154

CHAPTER 8   **Paul and the Church**   157
                 CHAPTER 8 REVIEW QUESTIONS   173

CHAPTER 9   **Paul and Meeting Human Needs**   175
                 CHAPTER 9 REVIEW QUESTIONS   192

CHAPTER 10   **Paul and the Birthing**   195
                 CHAPTER 10 REVIEW QUESTIONS   210

CHAPTER 11   **Paul and Spiritual Growth**   213
                 CHAPTER 11 REVIEW QUESTIONS   223

CHAPTER 12   **Paul and Eschatology**   225
                 CHAPTER 12 REVIEW QUESTIONS   241

More Christ-life Books   243
More Christ-life Booklets   244

And Stephen, full of faith and power, did great wonders
and miracles among the people. Then there arose certain
of the synagogue ... disputing with Stephen ... And [Ste-
phen] said, Behold, I see the heavens opened, and the Son
of man standing on the right hand of God. Then they cried
out with a loud voice, and stopped their ears, and ran upon him with one accord, and cast him out of the city, and
stoned him: and the witnesses laid down their clothes at a
young man's feet, whose name was Saul. And Saul was
consenting unto his death. (Acts 6:8–9; 7:56–58; 8:1)

FORWARD

This book is intended to arouse and strengthen the believer who wants to grow in the knowledge God gave Paul as the final gospel. Modern religion is geared to bring the believer to a certain place in understanding and stops there because that is as far as the doctrines go where believers are being taught. In this book, *religion* is defined as the teaching of self-effort for God's acceptance—anything one does within himself to please God—as opposed to accepting the unearned, free gift of God's grace through His sacrifice of His own Son. This book explores the truth that no human can please the Father with his own works; only Christ can please the Father, and that Christ is resident in every believer. He is our only hope of glory (Col. 1:27).

And Saul, yet breathing out threatenings and slaughter against the disciples of the Lord, went unto the high priest, and desired of him letters to Damascus to the synagogues, that if he found any of this way, whether they were men or women, he might bring them bound unto Jerusalem. (Acts 9:1–2)

PREFACE

The Story of Paul

Paul was born in Tarsus, the capital of the Province of Cilicia, a region that came to be known as Asia Minor. Most scholars place his birth at around A.D. 1 and his death at A.D. 68. Paul's Jewish parents were Roman citizens. Scholars are not certain how his parents came to acquire their Roman citizenship, but there is little reason to doubt Luke's suggestion (Acts 22:25–29; 23:27) that Paul inherited this status from his parents.

The history of the city of Tarsus shows it was absorbed into the Roman Empire in 66 B.C. As the political wheel of fortune turned with Mark Anthony's rise to power in 41 B.C., the city was granted freedom and immunity from taxation. According to practice in the Roman Empire, important people of a city who supported the incoming ruling power were given Roman citizenship as a reward for their support. Perhaps this is how Paul's parents received the citizenship they passed on to their son. Between 18 B.C. and A.D. 14, the number of Roman citizens in Tarsus increased by almost one million.

Despite its Roman status, Tarsus was more Eastern than Western in dress and in music. Its roots went back to the Empire of the Hittites in the third millennium B.C. In the first century, it was a well-governed, relatively prosperous city with Hellenic respect for education. Tarsus had the ability to equip its citizens to face both east and west and to function competently in both worlds. Paul benefited from that heritage.

In addition to being Roman citizens, Paul's family was most likely financially well-to-do; therefore, he probably received educational opportunities generally not available to the poor. There is no doubt that he was the most educated person in the Bible. In addition to Hellenic schools, he was also trained in the Hebrew school associated with the local synagogue. In Jewish families, religious education was obligatory through age 12. Paul knew both the Hebrew language and the Torah, although he appears to have read the Hebrew Scriptures primarily in the Greek version called the *Septuagint*. His letters contain no less than 90 citations from the Septuagint. He seems to have mastered oratorical skills, which were considered to be the key to advancement in his world. Oratory, in his day, was based on letter-writing and the study of speeches. The letters would actually be written as speeches designed to be read aloud to a public assembly. Paul even indicated that he expected his letters to be used in this manner in the assembly (2 Cor. 3:2; Col. 4:16; 1 Thess. 5:27; 1 Tim. 4:13). This form of communication, called epistles, reflects Paul's style. Although Paul liked to denigrate his speaking ability (1 Cor. 1:17; 2:4), the fact remains that his writing style is powerful. Also, he wrote epistles because he was unable to stay long periods of time in any one place because of the opposition of the Jews from Jerusalem.

The family in which Paul was raised, according to an abundance of biblical statements, strictly observed its Jewish heritage. Paul's passion for the traditions of Judaism reflected the value system he was taught in his home. Paul said he was *"circumcised the eighth day."* He described himself as a Pharisee in terms of the law and as *"blameless"* in terms of righteousness that came by the law (Acts 23:6; Phil. 3:4–6). It would be unlikely for him to acquire this level of commitment to the faith of his forefathers had he not been born into a family that valued this faith and practiced it with devotion. It is safe to assume there was a synagogue in

Tarsus with a Hebrew school. This school, apparently, was an important part of young Paul's life.

There was also a custom among the dispersed Jews of the Empire that two drachmas would be paid annually by every male for the support of the Temple in Jerusalem. One would imagine Paul's family made that contribution with enthusiasm. The Jewish people of the Diaspora never ceased to be citizens of two worlds: the nation in which they were physically domiciled and their spiritual home, which was centered in Jerusalem, specifically in the Temple.

Paul was a citizen of the first century who straddled the Jewish world and the Mediterranean world. It is fair to say that he, like all of us, was shaped by the cultural attitudes of his time, as there is no such thing as a universal human being. There is only the life of a particular person residing in a particular moment of history who accepts the values and definitions of his or her era and processes reality through the knowledge available during that period of history. To read Paul's writings accurately, one must understand him as he was, a citizen of his century whose life was marked by moments of great spiritual power and by moments of an unbelievable knowledge of what makes a human being tick. Because of that knowledge, he could be considered the greatest psychologist who ever lived. He was the first to know that God completed a human being by the rebirthing of another person, Christ, in the human (Col. 2:10). He was also the first in Christianity to see that the human being was tripartite—body, soul, and spirit (1 Thess. 5:23). Then he took this knowledge much deeper when he said a rebirthed believer should separate soul and spirit to understand the Christ-life (Heb. 4:12).

Those who read Paul's writings today need to appreciate these realities and seek to understand Paul's genius in terms of the limited psychological understanding that was available in his day. No one living today could transcend the knowledge that came to him by the revelation of Jesus Christ as the life of the human. Today, most believers—with all their so-called advanced learning—still miss what is plainly written in Paul's epistles.

According to Luke in the book of Acts, Paul's parents gave their son the Hebrew name Saul. Paul stated he was a member of the tribe of Benjamin (Phil. 3:5). In that tribe, the name Saul had a special history. Saul, the son of Kish, of the tribe of Benjamin, had been chosen to be the first king of the Jewish nation (1 Sam. 9). He had been selected, according to the biblical text, because of his imposing physical characteristics. Not only was he handsome, but *"from his shoulders and upward he was higher than any of the people"* (1 Sam. 9:2). Jewish biblical history, however, did not paint King Saul heroically. Indeed, he was portrayed as a melancholy, tragic figure whose depression had to be soothed with music and who flew into rages that suggested the probability of mental illness (1 Sam. 16:14–23). King Saul also lost the political support of the prophet Samuel, who according to the sacred story had been the king-maker in the first place. So Saul's royal line was not to be established. The end of Saul's reign as king was precipitated when Samuel, acting for God, found and anointed a replacement. God's choice was David, a young man not from the sons of the tribe of Benjamin, but rather from the tribe of Judah (1 Sam. 16:6–13). This act set into motion the inevitable conflict over the ownership of the royal line, which David finally won. Yet, the name Saul was still honored among the people of Israel and most especially among the people of the tribe of Benjamin, for whom it always projected an impressive image. Perhaps, the Benjamite background of Paul's parents was the reason they decided to choose Saul for their son's Hebrew name.

Paul's physical appearance apparently coincided with the Paulus (meaning "little") connotation of his name rather than the King Saul image. Though we cannot be absolutely certain of Paul's physical characteristics, there are hints that his stature and demeanor were not king-like. From Paul's own writings, we find one descriptive verse where he has repeated a critic's charge in order to refute it. His enemies had said of him, *"For his letters ... are weighty and powerful; but his bodily presence is weak, and his speech contemptible"* (2 Cor. 10:10).

It is interesting to note that Paul's defense against this charge consisted of his refutation of only half of that criticism. Paul wrote, *"But though I be rude in speech, yet not in knowledge"* (2 Cor. 11:6). It is not too great a leap to suggest that he made no defense against the other half of this charge because he knew that he was not a powerful bodily presence.

Luke, in the book of Acts, reinforced this autobiographical idea when he related a story of how the people of Lystra mistook Barnabas and Paul for gods. Barnabas, who appeared to be an imposing physical presence, was identified with Jupiter (Zeus, the king of the gods), while Paul was identified with Mercurius (Hermes, the messenger god) in Acts 14:1–18. Hermes was normally depicted in that society as a small, wiry, quick, and verbal deity. Although this does not constitute strong proof in our quest to be able to envision this important character in God's plan, it does add to the increasing possibility that this sense of small physical size was an accurate portrayal of Paul of Tarsus.

Another confirming source can be found in late second-century historical documents entitled The Acts of Paul and Thecla. There we find the first overt description of Paul from a physical point of view. He was referred to as being small in stature, bald-headed, bow-legged, and vigorous with meeting eyebrows and a slightly hooked nose. This source is not definitive, but it does suggest that no attempt had been made to transform Paul's physical characteristics to correspond to his enhanced stature in the Christian community of that day. The historical documents also continue the ongoing impression that Paul's stature did not constitute a dominating idea. Indeed, he might well have been susceptible to having the name Paulus applied to him in a mean, but not unheard-of way. Perhaps that is why the suggestion has been made that Paul used his Jewish name, Saul, only among Jews, where the connotations of the Greek adjective Paulus were not present, but he used the name Paul when he was among Greek-speaking Gentiles. There is also the suggestion that his family, who would need to give their son both a Jewish name and a Roman name, chose Paul because it came closest in their minds to the Hebrew name Saul.

It must be noted that nowhere in the Pauline Scriptures does Paul ever use any name but Paul. The suggestion that his name was also Saul comes to us exclusively from the writings of Luke in the book of Acts (See chapter 9.). No indication can be found that Luke had any motive in this matter except to relate a fact he knew to be true. So it seems reasonable to assume that the name Saul was used among the Jews, and the name Paul, among the Gentiles.

Following the custom among the upper class of Tarsus, Paul was sent abroad to complete his educational process. That custom brought him to Jerusalem at some point prior to the twentieth year of his life. It is estimated that he was in Jerusalem for about 15 years before his famous conversion experience when he met Christ on the road to Damascus. These were crucial years in Paul's development. His unusual zeal for the traditions of his forefathers enabled Paul to reach rare heights of excellence as a student. He was acclaimed and praised by his superiors. The force that led him into the position of persecutor of the Jewish-Christian community had been his dedication to keeping his religious traditions pure. His greatest desire was to be a member of the elite Sanhedrin, and it is said that he sought letters from the high priest to prosecute the followers of Jesus to gain attention from these Jewish leaders. Because it is inevitable that one draws near to that which one persecutes, Paul, the persecutor, clearly drew near to the Christian faith, and in time God chose him to be His apostle to the Gentiles. The irony of God was that He chose the meanest man on earth to be the recipient and messenger of grace.

Interestingly enough, Paul never describes his conversion experience in any of his epistles. It remained for Luke to give the narrative form in the book of Acts. While Paul did not write about his Damascus-road conversion, he writes liberally of the revelation of Christ in him which he received from God about three years later while in Arabia (Gal. 1:17). In fact, the in-Christ message was the root and base of his entire ministry. This revelation meant that Paul, the persecutor of the believers in the early Church, wanted acceptance by those he had previously victimized. It was not easy for Paul to enter into this new faith community—a community that was heavily imbued with the kingdom message of the Old Testament, a message focused on the restoration of the earthly kingdom through Israel's Messiah, Jesus of Nazareth.

Paul seemed to be sensitive to this belief and these feelings and did not force himself upon the Christians in Jerusalem. Instead, he felt a distinct call to be the apostle of grace to the Gentiles. He went to Arabia and stayed there three years (Gal. 1:18) while he received a revelation of Christ in him as his life. This revelation proved to be the greatest work of God in completing humans, whom He had already created in His likeness and image. It was the essence of the final and most important gospel, the gospel of grace. The fact that a born-again believer would hold another life, the Christ-life, would be information that could only come from the Father by the Holy Spirit. According to Paul's own account, he then went up to Jerusalem to confer for 15 days with Peter, the apostle, and James, the Lord's half-brother (Gal. 1:18–19). After that, he stayed in the region of Syria and Cilicia for 14 years (Gal. 1:21). He most likely spent those years with Barnabas in missionary service. He made a second journey to Jerusalem to deal with the issue of how Gentiles were to be incorporated into the predominantly Jewish-Christian community. Paul went to Jerusalem, this time accompanied by Barnabas and his only Greek assistant, Titus (Gal. 2:1). In Paul's mind a solution was worked out at that meeting, which resulted in Barnabas and Paul going to the Gentiles while James (not Christ's half-brother), Cephas, and John were to lead the mission to the Jews. The Jews were not to be freed from the demands of the law; however, the Gentiles were not to be bound by the demands of the law. It was a difficult solution for Paul (Gal. 2:2–10).

Paul returned to his missionary activities, splitting his next two years between Philippi and Thessalonica as an official representative of the Antioch church. Unfortunately, Judaizers from Jerusalem, in violation of the Jerusalem agreement, continued to press Paul's congregations to adhere to various elements of the law. Paul felt his gospel being compromised by the encroaching demands of a new legalism. The church at Antioch seemed to be sinking back into being a Jewish church. That was intolerable for Paul, so he launched into a more Gentile-oriented western missionary tour. His primary tie with the East from that day forward consisted of his commitment to collect an offering for the support of the Jerusalem church. Thus, his orbit of missionary work kept stretching farther and farther west.

Paul developed a unique missionary style once he was on his own. He developed a central office in a region; then he developed a process to visit, establish, build, and encourage the churches of that region with regularity. Corinth, Ephesus, and Rome were his three primary centers or headquarters during the course of his career. Paul, like every church leader, had different problems with different churches. Possibly the church in Corinth tested him the most with its internal disorders. Philippi was perhaps the church toward which he felt the most affection.

During his life, Paul worked with a number of close associates. Timothy seems to have been his primary assistant; however, he also mentions with frequency Titus, Apollo, Silvanus, and a couple named Priscilla and Aquila. Priscilla and Aquila were probably more important to Paul's missionary success than anyone has yet imagined. This couple appears to have constituted Paul's advance team, moving in and setting up headquarters in all three of Paul's centers of activity in anticipation of his arrival (Rom. 16:3; 1 Cor. 16:19; 2 Tim. 4:19).

Paul fought vigorously to keep his churches from being dragged back into the legalism of Judaism, which was a compromise of the true gospel. The gospel of grace and the truth that Christ lives in the believer burned in him too greatly to have it commingled with law and legalism. This erroneous teaching of law and legalism was a regular part of his battle in seeking to establish Gentile churches. His letters are filled with vigorous defenses of his apostleship, of his understanding of the gospel of grace, and of the Gentile mission of the Church.

The book of Acts records three primary missionary journeys Paul took, but there is a considerable distinction between the chronicle found in the book of Acts and the one we discern from reading Paul's own words. Christian scholarship almost always sides with Paul when there is a conflict with the book of Acts. Paul is, after all, writing a first-person account. The book of Acts is a well-after-the-fact narrative. In any event, the final phase of Paul's life appears to have been under arrest and in chains in the city of Rome in the A.D. 60s. He lived there under house arrest, and the evidence is that he died there as a Christian martyr.

The Gospel of Paul

Paul left a legacy for the future of Christianity, the value of which cannot be overestimated. When Paul died, three of the four Gospels had not yet been written. Matthew was probably written the year Paul died. This makes Paul the primary witness to the nature of primitive Christianity, and he gave the final message of God to humans based on Ephesians 1:4, that we were chosen to be in Christ before the world was created. Paul's epistles were formal documents to be read in the assembly of the faithful as teaching instruments. His first letters are 1 and 2 Thessalonians, which are generally dated between A.D. 52 and 53.

Galatians is also an early Pauline letter and is dated around A.D. 53. This letter expresses the pain Paul felt when the Judaizers challenged him and threatened to undercut his work. He fought vigorously to protect the true gospel and the churches for which he was responsible. The Epistle to the Galatians is Paul at his pugilistic best. Here he writes the words, *"I withstood him* [Peter] *to the face, because he was to be blamed* [condemned]*"* (Gal. 2:11, author's words added). These were certainly the words needed then, as they are now; for most believers in the modern churches of today are bound by the same law and legalistic element.

First and Second Corinthians are also authentic Pauline works. One section found in 2 Corinthians chapters 10–13 reveals Paul to be so powerful that he raises his voice more than ever against the religious forces of the day.

Romans is the only letter Paul wrote to a church he had not founded. However, he did hope to visit Rome, so he wrote this epistle to spell out his understanding of the gospel as God had given it to him. The Epistle to the Romans follows a similar argument to the one that first appeared in the Epistle to the Galatians. Romans, however, is more formal and more magnificent than Galatians. So complete and passionate is this piece of literature that many refer to this epistle as "the gospel according to Paul." Chapters 1–8 contain Paul's basic understanding of the function of the Christ-life. In chapters 9–11, Paul discusses the place of the Jews in the drama of salvation and this new gospel of grace. Finally, in chapters 12–15, Paul draws the ethical implications that are present in the true gospel. God allowed him to call all his writings "my gospel."

It is important to note that the first seven epistles Paul wrote (1 and 2 Thessalonians, 1 and 2 Corinthians, Romans, Galatians, and Hebrews), were all written in the Acts period, sometime between Acts 13 and Acts 28. In each of these epistles he appealed to the Jews to accept Christ; and to those who already believed, he taught the rudiments of the Christ-life.

His next seven epistles are Ephesians, Philippians, Colossians, 1 and 2 Timothy, Titus, and Philemon. These epistles deal with the outworking of Christ as He lives in the believer.

The Epistle to Philemon is a tender letter commending a runaway slave, Onesimus, to his former master and is revelatory on many levels. The Epistle to the Philippians is thought by some to be the most personal Pauline letter. It contains many memorable passages, and at least one section appears to reflect an early Christian hymn (Phil. 2:5–11). This passage reveals some fascinating aspects in the early development of the in-Christ message. On the one hand, it introduces the divine pre-existence of Jesus; and on the other hand, it moves directly from crucifixion to exaltation.

There is no way Philippians, Colossians, and Ephesians can be separated. They are not only prison epistles, but they are the heart and breath of Paul's revelation of Christ in the believer. The Pastoral Epistles of 1 and 2 Timothy and Titus are generally considered as structure for the believer's daily walk in Christ.

The Epistle to the Hebrews is Pauline, despite the fact that many contest it. The King James Bible once proclaimed it "The Epistle of Paul to the Hebrews." Although its style and vocabulary are not the same as Paul's other writings, its general message fits Paul, and no one else has surfaced as its author. Once again, it is Paul attempting to bring Israel into the Christian Church.

Anyone who pulls together Paul's major teachings, as revealed in his own writings, must begin with the truth that sin is an internal power (sin-nature) or force that separated human life from God. Sin entered human life through Adam and enslaved the entire world. It constituted a massive disorientation of God's purpose. Paul's response to this status of sin was to focus on the power of God's grace, which was fully revealed in the sacrifice of Christ. As a result of the Cross, a total rebirth of the human being would be required. The law of the Jews, the Torah, could never have anticipated the gift of God, which was the rebirthing of human beings, fully and finally recreated as offspring of God, the Father. The work of Christ on the cross removed the dogmatic claims of the law upon the Jewish people.

Self-sacrificing love, as revealed in Christ, is a portrait of what authentic humanity should be. Paul saw this love revealed in Christ—who did not please Himself but suffered on behalf of human beings— dying even for the godless. Christ's love is so total that nothing can separate us from the love of God that is in Christ Jesus (Rom. 8:38–39). For this self-sacrificing love, God has exalted Jesus, and *"given him a name which is above every name: That at the name of Jesus every knee should bow"* (Phil. 2:5–11).

We who are in Christ are called to live that grace-filled life by living with the same self-sacrificing love of Christ in us. Christ in us was the essence of Paul's revelation in the Arabian Desert and the essence of the grace of God. For Paul, God's greatest gift to the world was Christ in the believer as the believer's only life. That far surpassed the gift of the law or anything else the Father had ever done before.

Paul was content to give his life, his energy, and his devotion for this gospel. For his service to the Lord he willingly endured incredible abuse, beatings, shipwrecks, danger from robbers on land, storms at sea, and, finally, death (2 Cor. 11:23–29). Paul was convinced, *"For to me to live is Christ, and to die is gain"* (Phil. 1:21). This statement is a tremendous witness of one who fully loved the Lord.

The Message of Paul

The preceding discussion is a brief description of the life and ministry of Paul, but the impact of the revelation of Christ in him is a rather different story. Paul left information in his epistles from which we may understand the inner man, which is Christ in the believer. This is the greatest truth God ever gave to mortals, aside from the plan of redemption. Anyone who can read will see the simplicity of God's final gospel clearly taught in Paul's writings.

Because of Paul's importance to the plan of God and the divine inspiration attributed to his words, the Church should build its creeds and doctrines on his letters. Instead, the humanity of Paul (Christ in him) has remained hidden in the shadows, covered by layers of piety, fear, manmade religion, and repression. It is my conviction that Paul's Christ-humanity provides the clue to understanding everything he did and everything he wrote, and it is imperative that the Christ in Paul be searched and studied as the main theme of the Christian life.

I see Paul as a zealot, teaching the truth of Christ in him based on the Arabian revelation the Father gave him. That revelation is easy to document because he acknowledges it himself (Gal. 1:11–14). One does not erupt in such fury, as noted in Galatians 1, unless zealotry has been part of the person for a long time. He describes himself in verse 14 as zealous for the law, as eager to move beyond all of his peers in devotion to his studies.

Godly fury, properly understood, is a means and a method of survival. In every age, God has had some believers who are this way. They cannot tolerate those who might question the truth or the authenticity of what they have been taught by the Spirit. Paul, as a young man studying in his synagogue school, must have manifested these characteristics. When he moved to Jerusalem—the city where religious devotion was standard—these tendencies probably were accelerated. Paul took second place to no one in piety, devotion, and zeal. Yet, the religious practices he adopted were more and more those of rigid control. Before his conversion, he was out attempting to destroy anyone who followed Jesus of Nazareth.

Paul possessed *"a thorn in the flesh"* that he called *"the messenger of Satan"* (2 Cor. 12:7). Suggestions have abounded throughout history as to what this "thorn" consisted of. While there has been agreement on a specific explanation, it is fair to say that the weight of scholarship seeking answers has fastened on some type of physical ailment. Suggestions have included epilepsy, poor eyesight, a chronic eye infection, recurring fevers, or a speech impediment. Yet, none of these proposed explanations seem to be convincing when one considers the physical rigor of Paul's life. He walked to most of the cities on his journeys, sometimes traveling for weeks or months at a time. He slept on roadsides or in inns and ate whatever food he could find. It is difficult to conceive of Paul having a serious physical malady that would haunt him and still do the physical things that we know he did.

When we combine the physical explanations to the spiritual, a richer and more truthful set of possibilities emerges. Verse 7 says the thorn in the flesh was given because of his revelation of Christ in the believer. It is obvious that Paul had received information from God that no one else in God's administration had ever received. The thorn in the flesh was an act of God to protect His message of perfect grace and the revelation of Jesus Christ in the human.

What did Paul say that gives us a clue to his conversion? He told us nothing about a Damascus-road experience. He never mentioned Ananias, who tended to him and baptized him. All these stories are narratives in Acts. Paul had no chance to speak about their authenticity. Paul did say conversion meant he had been joined to Christ and all converted ones are "in Christ" and belong to Christ (1 Cor. 1:30; 3:23). He did say if we are "beside ourselves," it is for God (2 Cor. 5:13). He insisted that Christ died for all so that all might live for Him and in Him (v. 15). He insisted that our old self was crucified with Christ and united with Him in resurrection (Rom. 6:5–6). He considered himself dead to sin but alive to God (Rom. 6:11). He asserted that sin no longer dwelt in his body to make him obey its passions (v. 12). He proclaimed that once his *"members"* were slaves to impurity, but they became *"servants to righteousness"* (Rom. 6:19). He said, *"I am apprehended of Christ Jesus"* (Phil. 3:12). He said nothing could separate him from the love of God (Rom. 8:39), and the love of God controlled him (2 Cor. 5:14). He declared that no one who believes in Christ shall be put to shame (Rom. 10:11).

What was the scriptural content of Paul's conversion? Since Paul did not relate that experience directly, we can only evaluate the effects of his conversion as stated in the Scriptures. Speaking of his own conversion he wrote, *"I knew a man in Christ above fourteen years ago (whether in the body, I cannot tell; or whether out of the body, I cannot tell: God knoweth;) such a one caught up to the third heaven"* (2 Cor. 12:2). When one turns to God, the veil shall be taken away (2 Cor. 3:16). He was alluding to his conversion when he said, *"For God ... hath shined in our hearts, to give the light of the knowledge of the glory of God in the face of Jesus Christ"* (2 Cor. 4:6). Paul believed he had been given the grace of the life of Christ. It was not his doing; it was God's gracious act. It convinced him that there was no condemnation, not only for him but also for all *"which are in Christ Jesus"* (Rom. 8:1). In a very revealing way he asserted that even his flesh could never separate him from the love of God. In that respect, he pronounced himself more than a conqueror *"through him that loved us"* (Rom. 8:35–37).

Conversion came while he was journeying to Damascus. *"Suddenly there shined round about him a light from heaven: and he fell to the earth, and heard a voice"* (Acts 9:3–4). The voice was, *"Jesus whom thou persecutest"* (v. 5). Those traveling with him saw nothing (v. 7). Paul also saw nothing, as he was blinded, and so he was led by the hand to Damascus. For three days he lived in darkness, neither eating nor drinking (vv. 8–9). His restoration was to be reminiscent, at least in time, of the resurrection of his Lord, who also lived in darkness, the darkness of death, for three days.

By way of a vision, he received word that Ananias would come to restore his sight. When Ananias arrived, Luke wrote that scales seemed to fall from Paul's eyes. He was then baptized and filled with the Holy Spirit (Acts 9:10–19).

That was Luke's version of what occurred in Paul when his enormous inner conflict of sin was finally resolved. Paul discovered that his fears, his dark side, and his unacceptable desires were now known by God and done away with by the Cross of Christ. He was now accepted, loved, and transformed. The great mystery—which is Christ in us (Col. 1:27)—had been performed by the miracle of being born again. He had been baptized into Christ and invited into God's love, as the hymn says, "Just as I am, without one plea" (Charlotte Elliott, 1835). The love of God made known in Christ had embraced him. The inner turmoil of sin was resolved. Paul was set free from the old sin-nature. He was now free to live, free to love, and free to be who God created him to be because Christ had made him His own (Phil. 3:12).

This would be the pattern all men would follow to be free from sin and be what God wanted them to be. Finally, Paul would say, *"Be ye followers of me, even as I also am of Christ"* (1 Cor. 11:1). In Paul, God had found His champion of grace. Paul would be the vessel God would use to bring the message of the rebirthing to all who believe on the Lord Jesus Christ. This one man would be the means of a message the Father would use to fill His house with His own offspring.

When Paul died, he left behind the only written record of how God's birthed offspring should live. He lived and died bringing to all grace and the mystery, *"Christ in you, the hope of glory"* (Col. 1:27).

And as he journeyed, he came near Damascus: and suddenly there shined round about him a light from heaven: And he fell to the earth, and heard a voice saying unto him, Saul, Saul, why persecutest thou me? And he said, Who art thou, Lord? And the Lord said, I am Jesus whom thou persecutest: it is hard for thee to kick against the pricks. (Acts 9:3–5)

CHAPTER 1
Paul and the Gentiles

Introduction

I believe many people don't understand the significance of what took place in Acts 28 and its
importance in God's plan for the born-again believer.

> *And when they agreed not among themselves,
> they departed, after that Paul had spoken one
> word, Well spake the Holy Ghost by Isaiah the
> prophet unto our fathers, Saying, Go unto this
> people, and say, Hearing ye shall hear, and
> shall not understand; and seeing ye shall see,
> and not perceive: for the heart of this people
> is waxed gross, and their ears are dull of
> hearing, and their eyes have they closed; lest
> they should see with their eyes, and hear with
> their ears, and understand with their heart,
> and should be converted, and I should heal
> them.* (Acts 28:25–27)

These verses are talking about the Jews who were in a
meeting with Paul. When the Jews *"agreed not among
themselves, they departed, after that Paul had spoken
one word."* When they had disagreements, they got up
and left. The terminology here does not mean he gave
them one single word. It means that he gave them the
Word. What was the Word that Paul gave to these Israelites? *"Well spake the Holy Ghost by Esaias* [Isaiah]
the prophet unto our fathers." Paul gave to these Jews
the passage from Isaiah 6:9–10. Paul did not give it in
his own words; he gave it as it came through the
prophet Isaiah! Paul wanted Israel to know what was

about to take place should not come as a surprise to them because of what Isaiah had to say in this regard 700 years earlier. Paul said, *The one word I am giving to you comes from Isaiah, and this is what he said: "Go unto this people, and say, hearing ye shall hear, and shall not understand; and seeing ye shall see, and not perceive."* He told them a time would come when Israel would see and hear but not understand, and a day was coming when they would not grasp anything God was doing.

What God Did for Israel

God sent His Son as a babe in Bethlehem to restore Israel. When Jesus began His ministry, He said to the apostles, *"But go rather to the lost sheep of the house of Israel"* (Matt. 10:6). The primary ministry of Jesus of Nazareth was to Israel. Everything Jesus said had to do with restoring Israel. On the Day of Pentecost and throughout the 36-year period of the book of Acts, Israel missed what Jesus came to earth to do for them. Jesus had come to earth working signs, wonders, and miracles in order to turn Israel to God; and they did not see it, nor did they hear it. Isaiah had said the day would come when God would not deal with Israel any longer. Look at what God had done for Israel. He had their King come to Bethlehem through a miracle to sit on David's throne. He had their King die on Calvary for them. He sent the Holy Spirit to introduce them to Jesus, and they missed it all! Verse 27 of Acts 28 tells us why this had happened. *"For the heart of this people [Israel] is waxed gross, and their ears are dull of hearing, and their eyes have they closed."* They cannot see, hear, or feel the things of God any longer.

Verse 28 is the key to this entire passage. This verse starts with *"be it known,"* which is a legal statement. *"Be it known therefore unto you, that the salvation of God is sent unto the Gentiles, and that they will hear it."* So profound is this verse that two-thirds of the Bible is eclipsed by this statement. Everything written in the Bible from Genesis 12 to Acts 28 was overwhelmed, literally pushed aside, and will not be honored by God as far as salvation goes until Jesus comes back a second time to establish His earthly kingdom.

God's Message to Israel

In Genesis 12, God called a man by the name of Abram (Abraham) out of Ur of the Chaldees and made a promise that his seed was going to number the sand of the seashore and the stars of the heavens. He said Abraham was going to be the father of a new nation. You must remember in the Scriptures there are only three races of people as far as God is concerned. There is the Gentile race, the Jewish race, and the new-creation race (2 Cor. 5:16–17; Gal. 3:26–29; 6:15; Col. 3:10–11), which are the born-again believers. There are only three races of people to God because there are only three predominant fathers in the Bible. The father of the Gentiles is Adam. The father of Israel is Abraham. The father of the born-again is our Heavenly Father.

It is important that you understand the fact that nationality, ethnicity, tribal affiliation, or any other group you want to identify with does not matter in God's plan. Not even Jews and Gentiles ultimately matter in God's plan because three times Paul said when you are born again, or are in Christ, you are no longer Jew or Gentile (Rom. 10:12; Gal. 3:28; Col. 3:11). Neither the Gentile nor the Jewish race survives being born again! The plan of God is not that Jews or Gentiles should reign. The plan of God is that you must be born again! You must be of the race that God fathers.

God is saying in these verses that the day has come when everything He had said to Israel is being temporarily set aside. When God called Abraham out of Ur of the Chaldees and said he was going to be the father of a new nation, God dealt with the one race of people birthed by Abraham, and that is exactly what He did for the next 1,700 years of biblical history. For these 1,700 years, there had been a message for Israel. That message was that if you repent and do what God tells you to do, you will rule over the land. Israel never did that.

The Gospel of Self-effort

What is it about repentance and water baptism that is different from grace? Repentance and water baptism are things you do! When Jesus died on the cross, and once the transition between law and grace was completed, He would never again accept repentance and water baptism as the means of salvation because those are things you do. After the Cross, salvation became a matter of simply believing on the finished work of Christ at Calvary. Acts 16:31 is the first time this change was introduced, *"Believe on the Lord Jesus Christ, and thou shalt be saved."* A whole new gospel coming out of the book of Acts that did not belong to the Jews was emerging here. What the Jews called the gospel of Moses, and later was called by Paul the gospel of circumcision, was actually a gospel of self-effort. To this day, the Judaistic message centers on self-effort. Multitudes in Christianity have adopted that same gospel of self-effort, believing there is something they can do to be saved or to stay saved, to the ignorance of what Christ did for them and as them on the cross. Instead of Christ on the cross being their complete means of salvation, religion continues to add repentance and water baptism as conditions for salvation.

Different Ways God Has Worked with People

Before Genesis 12, we have the longest time period in the Bible. From Adam to Abraham covers more than 2,300 years. During that period of time, there were four dispensations. These dispensations are four different ways God dealt with humanity in the first 12 chapters of Genesis. Those four dispensations are the Dispensation of Innocence, the Dispensation of Conscience, the Dispensation of Human Government, and finally, the Dispensation of Promise.

All human beings up until Genesis 12 were of the seed of Adam. All of these people were Gentiles. Abraham, who came out of Ur of the Chaldees, was a Gentile. By Genesis 12, God showed that no group of people had it within themselves to obey Him. He could not leave it up to man's free will to please Him. What God did through Abraham was to raise up an entirely new kingdom, a whole new nation called Israel that came out of Jacob. God proclaimed this nation would be the only people He would deal with. From Abraham to the Apostle Paul, Israel was the primary people God dealt with.

Four-fifths of the Bible deals with the people who have very little to do with Gentiles. They are another family, a different nation, and they have a different father. I make this point because all our lives we have been taught from the four-fifths of the Scriptures written to Israel mixed with the one-fifth that pertains to us, the born-again. On the one hand, this has made us believe that God is the one who accomplishes things, like He did for Israel, while on the other hand we believe if we don't get busy and do things, then nothing will be accomplished. We become comminglers, mixing self-effort and grace, not knowing the difference between the two.

In Acts 28, God moved to a new family of people, the new-creation race (2 Cor. 5:17). When Paul stood before Israel and said the day had come where Israel is blind, deaf, and rejecting God's plan, a new phase of God's plan emerged. A new group of people was going to be dealt with, who had never before been dealt with, especially in the Scriptures. You must realize that from the time God began to work with Abraham, His entire interest was in Israel. From Genesis 12 to Acts 28, Jews were the prime group of people to God. Occasionally, there was a Gentile here and there and a nation here and there that was blessed of the Lord. God blessed them because He wanted to "spank" Israel, so God gave them power as they came against Israel. Never during this time did the plan of God belong to the Gentiles.

You may recall that Jesus of Nazareth called His disciples together and told them to preach that the kingdom was going to be established on earth. His instructions were to go only to the lost sheep of the house of Israel. The disciples were not to go to the Gentiles. Later, Jesus did minister to some Gentiles as a bridge to show the grace of God that was necessary to begin the transition from law to grace. However, the message during the earthly ministry of Jesus was not to the Gentiles. You may remember the reaction of Jesus to the Syrophenician woman, in Mark 7:24–30. We read in that account that Jesus said, *"It is not meet* [good] *to take the children's bread, and to cast it unto the dogs."* Jesus referred to the Gentiles as dogs!

We should also look at what God had to do in the book of Acts to Peter in order to change his mind about Gentiles. Peter had a vision of a sheet let down of animals that he had never eaten before (Acts 10:9–16). God told Peter to take and eat of the unclean animals, a sign that Peter was to accept the people who were "dogs" (Gentiles). We know this is the meaning of the vision by reading Acts 10:28 and 34. This was very different for Peter, but under the command of the Lord, he went over to the home of Cornelius. After Peter arrived, he started preaching the only thing he knew, his regular law message, *"the word which God sent unto the children of Israel"* (Acts 10:36–37; 47–

48). Before Peter could finish his message, power fell on the group, and they all received the Holy Spirit just like what happened on the Day of Pentecost. This incident upset the Jews (Acts 11:1–3). God was beginning to cross over the bridge from law to the other side where grace was.

The Jewish Nation Today

The Jewish-Christian worker today really gets upset when I talk about the Jewish nation being set aside. Many of them don't understand the birthing or the "in-Christ" position of believers. They believe if they can entice the Jewish person to believe that all the types and shadows in the Old Testament point to their Messiah, and if they see their need of water baptism and repentance, then that person can be saved. I believe the only way Jews can be saved today is just as Gentiles are saved. They simply must believe on the Lord Jesus Christ. Through no work or effort of their own can they be saved.

Furthermore, Paul said three times that once a Jew is in Christ, he is no longer a Jew. What he becomes is a member of the new-creation race. That is what it means to be born again. When Gentiles are born again, they are no longer Gentile. There are no Germans in Christ, no Scotsmen, no Irish, and there are no Jews or Gentiles in Christ. We have a new father. We are a whole new race of people. We are different than anyone who has ever lived. If an African-American person is saved, he is no longer an African-American to God. If a Hispanic person is saved, he is no longer a Hispanic—he is part of a new race of people.

In the world today, people tell me they want to protect and preserve their culture, their past, and their native language, although many no longer use it. This is all contrary to the true gospel. It is not a question whether I want them to all speak English, or for that matter to be Texans. I want them to know what it means to be born again! In Christ we lose everything that has to do with the past, and Paul made that very plain. *"Therefore if any man be in Christ, he is a new creature: old things are passed away; behold, all things are become new"* (2 Cor. 5:17).

When the gospel is not preached, everyone ends up fighting and fussing over who and what he or she is. The gospel of the Dispensation of Grace is entirely different from the gospel Dispensation of Law, and it has nothing to do with the past. *"For if, when we were enemies, we were reconciled to God by the death of his Son, much more, being reconciled, we shall be saved by his life"* (Rom. 5:10). When we understand what Paul said here, we can see that we are saved by the life of Christ. Salvation is Christ in the believer, saving that believer by His life in the believer.

The Gospel to the Gentiles

What is the gospel that went to the Gentiles? It bothers me when people try to prove that the gospel of Jesus Christ that is meant for us today is found in the Old Testament. Do not misinterpret what I am saying; the entire Bible is the Word of God. It is God speaking to people. However, the way He spoke to people in certain places in certain circumstances and situations is not the way in which He deals with us today. If you look at the early Church, you can see that the law was still at work. An example would be when Ananias and Sapphira did not bring their gifts to the Lord according to the way they should have and they were struck dead by God (Acts 5:1–11). That was law at work! Under grace, God has put His Son in us and has let us know that we cannot live without Him. Ananias and Sapphira were dishonest. How many of us are like them today? But God does not strike us dead because we are under His grace. The Dispensation of Grace is an entirely new message.

When God called Abraham, He told him he was going to rule over earth. This kingdom message is an earthly message. The Jew is intended to rule over this earth, and he will do so in the Millennium. The children fathered by God (the born-again)—contrasted with the children fathered by Abraham—do not belong to this earth. We are ambassadors here for God right now, but we are an entirely different breed of people who belong in and are headed for the Father's house. Abraham, as the father of Israel, had an old message. It is a message that was set aside in Acts 28. The new gospel is that you must be born again because you must have a new father. You have an entirely new life. It is not your life though; it is the life of the Father's Son in you. We receive this gospel from the Apostle Paul.

My Gospel

There are three Scriptures you should mark in your Bible that will make a difference in your walk in God. *"In the day when God shall judge the secrets of men by Jesus Christ according to my gospel"* (Rom. 2:16) is the first. Circle the two words "my gospel." Those words are definitive. They are distinctive. They are different from anything anyone else said in the Bible. Circle these same words in Romans 16:25 and 2 Timothy 2:8.

In the New Testament there are a number of different gospels mentioned. One of these is referred to as the gospel of Moses or Moses' gospel. In Mark 1:1, we read of *"the gospel of Jesus Christ."* In Galatians 2:7, two gospels are mentioned, *"the gospel of circumcision"* and *"the gospel of uncircumcision."* The gospel of Moses and the gospel of circumcision are linked together and are practically the same thing. The gospel of Jesus Christ is that of Jesus of Nazareth ministering to Israel. That gospel was set aside when Jesus was translated back to heaven because that gospel was the gospel of the kingdom based on the messiahship of Jesus, which was rejected by Israel. That is why Jesus did not go to the Gentiles preaching the kingdom of heaven is at hand. That gospel was only for the lost sheep of the house of Israel.

Most people believe the only gospel in the New Testament is the gospel of Jesus Christ. There is a distinct difference between the gospel of Jesus Christ according to Matthew, Mark, Luke, and John, and the gospel of Jesus Christ according to Paul. The first gospel focused on Jesus on this earth and dealt with restoring the kingdom for the nation of Israel, which was to restore the earth. At this time Jesus was in an earthly body given to Him by Mary. The gospel Jesus preached at this time was given to an earthly people who would remain here on this earth.

The second gospel concerns Jesus who is seated at the right hand of the Father and deals with the Father birthing His own family. This gospel came from Jesus, the same Jesus, but He was in a different form. This second form was as God's eternally resurrected Son. The second gospel was given to Paul, and he was told this gospel has to do with believers seated in heavenly places. These are two entirely different gospels that cannot be mixed together or commingled without confusing results. A better way to put it could be to say that Jesus was a heavenly creature sent to an earthly people, Israel, to restore the earth; and Paul was an earthly creature sent by Christ to raise up a heavenly people to go on to the Father's house.

In Romans 2:16, I want you to see the distinctiveness of the gospel belonging to the Apostle Paul. So distinctive was it that he called it "my gospel." It was called "my gospel" because God gave to Paul; He had not given it to anyone else.

Romans 16:25 reads, *"Now to him that is of power to stablish you according to my gospel."* Here is the second mention of *"my gospel."* This is the gospel of

Jesus Christ according to the Apostle Paul. But, is this not the same gospel Jesus of Nazareth preached? No, it is not! When Paul said *"my gospel"* he made a severe distinction in the Scriptures. In 2 Corinthians 5:16, Paul said, *"Wherefore henceforth know we no man after the flesh: yea, though we have known Christ after the flesh, yet now henceforth know we him no more."* Christ was in the flesh when He was Jesus of Nazareth. The gospel He preached during that dispensation is not to new creation believers. The Christ we know is in a different form (spirit) and lives within us.

Paul's third mention of "my gospel" appears in 2 Timothy 2:8, *"Remember that Jesus Christ of the seed of David was raised from the dead according to my gospel."* Three times Paul said *"my gospel."* It is not Peter's gospel, and it is not a gospel out of the book of Isaiah. Paul said he is delivering to us a message God gave him in the Arabian Desert.

> *But when it pleased God, who separated me from my mother's womb, and called me by His grace, to reveal His Son in me, that I might preach Him among the heathen; immediately I conferred not with flesh and blood: Neither went I up to Jerusalem to them which were apostles before me; but I went into Arabia, and returned again unto Damascus.* (Gal. 1:15–17)

That was the gospel Paul taught—the revelation of the Jesus Christ who lives in the human being who believes in Him. The gospel that Paul said belongs to the Gentiles is a gospel of *"Christ in you, the hope of glory"* (Col. 1:27). This is the gospel of the mystery. It is Christ in you. You have God's nature in you (2 Peter 1:4). You have the life of the Son of God in you (1 John 5:12).

The Apostle Paul wrote, *"For I determined not to know any thing among you, save Jesus Christ, and him crucified"* (1 Cor. 2:2). It has taken me 40 years to understand what Paul meant by that statement, and I have concluded he meant that was the only thing he wanted to know. The statement had to do with who he was, how he lived, and what the gospel meant to him. That is the gospel to the Gentiles according to the Apostle Paul.

Chapter 1
Review Questions

1. All of us have an earthly father. The Bible reveals that we have another father in addition to our earthly (third-dimensional) father.

   a. Who is that father?

   b. Why do you say he is your father?

2. In Romans 10:12, Galatians 3:28, and Colossians 3:11, Paul states there is neither Jew nor Gentile. Explain what these statements mean to you.

3. In this chapter, the point is made that before the Cross, God had established repentance and water baptism as a means of salvation. After the Cross, grace was the means of salvation. What is the difference between these two sets of requirements?

4. Describe the people who were under each of the two different means of salvation in question #3.

5. What is your definition of a commingled gospel?

6. What are the disadvantages or problems with a commingled gospel?

7. How many gospels do you find in the Bible, and briefly explain each one?

*And Ananias went his way, and entered into the house;
and putting his hands on him said, Brother Saul, the
Lord, even Jesus, that appeared unto thee in the way as
thou camest, hath sent me, that thou mightest receive thy
sight, and be filled with the Holy Ghost. (Acts 9:17)*

CHAPTER 2
Paul and the Cross

Introduction

To Christians, the central theme of the Bible is the message of the Cross—that is, that Christ died on the cross to save sinners. It comes as quite a surprise to many believers then that the message of salvation through the death of Jesus Christ on Calvary's Cross was never preached until Paul received his revelation that Christ lives in the believer! Only after Paul had a revelation of Christ as the life of the human being (Gal. 2:20) did Christians begin to understand that salvation came through the Cross.

As we read the Old Testament, we find no clear reference to the Cross in it, unless we take our New Testament understanding back with us into the Old Testament Scriptures. Even Jesus of Nazareth did not preach the Cross or man's salvation through it. Jesus did talk about others taking up their cross and following Him in Matthew 16, Mark 8, and Luke 9. Jesus also told His disciples that the time had come for Him to suffer many things. However, Peter disagreed with what the Lord had said and rebuked Him. Peter was well versed in the kingdom message that Christ had only come to rule and reign on earth. Peter was looking for prosperity and health, and he did not believe there was room for suffering in the gospel, as he understood it at that time.

Have you ever met a kingdom person, someone who is caught up in the kingdom message and is unwilling to talk about suffering? These people will tell you that your negative thoughts are of the Devil and that you don't have to suffer as a Christian. They will tell you that if you only had enough faith, then you could be free of these erroneous thoughts about suffering.

Jesus went through the same thing when He talked of suffering. Peter acted as if Jesus had violated the kingdom message. Jesus was forced to say, *"Get thee behind me, Satan!"* (Matt. 16:23). Peter was denying the reality of the situation.

Who's Cross?

"Then said Jesus unto his disciples, If any man will come after me, let him deny himself, and take up his cross, and follow me" (Matt. 16:24). When we read this, we are left to ask ourselves: What cross was He talking about? Jesus was not talking about the cross upon which He would die, as there was no concept at that time that He was going to die on a cross! This was a colloquial expression of that time period. The Roman way of killing felons was by crucifixion, and the condemned were required to carry their own crosses. Jesus' comment was a cliché of that era. It would be the same as me saying to someone, *If you continue in your ways, you will end up going to the electric chair.*

When Jesus made this statement about *"carrying your cross,"* He was talking about hard times in their lives—just like criminals and others have a hard time bearing responsibility for the issues of life. Prior to Calvary, the individual had to take up his own cross. But now, in the Dispensation of Grace that followed Calvary, we no longer bear our own crosses. Instead, because of all He accomplished with His death, we are carried by His cross. We must fix it in our minds that we are now saved through grace. *amazing grace*

I had this truth illustrated to me some years ago by a woman who had spent many years in foreign missionary work. I had been preaching at a conference, and as the meeting was breaking up I stepped down into the auditorium and was met by a grey-haired woman. After introducing herself, she said she needed to talk with me for a moment. She said when she was young she met a young man who had just graduated from Bible college and who believed he had been called to the mission field. They fell in love, were married, and went to a foreign field. They had a wonderful life. God gave them a nice home, and they built many churches, set up training centers, and won souls to God. In the process of time, they had two sons who were raised on the mission field. One day, a terrible disease came across the land and her husband died. She said it was a big blow to their happy life, and she thought she would not survive. Her mission board sent word that she and the boys should come home, but she wrote and told them that by God's grace she would stay and carry on the work. The boys grew up and entered into the ministry with her, and the Lord blessed their work. Then, another awful disease came and her two boys died. She had now lost everything that was precious to her. Again, the mission board wrote for her to come home, but she stayed a few more years until her body began to fail, and finally, she had to go home. She told me the one thing she learned through all this was that whenever she had to go on, she had to pick up that cross on which she had died with Jesus and know that out of that death came life. God had taught her that if she had His cross fixed in her mind, when she needed help, His cross would carry her! The secret was in the Cross!

I must share with you that at one time I preached what is called the "deeper life message." That message promoted the belief that because Jesus died on the cross, every one of us can be free and happy. I preached that people had to make the cross work for them by picking up their crosses and doing something with them. I said they needed to read the Bible more, pray more, give more, or do more. That was the old deeper life message. The bottom line of the deeper life message was that you need to do something to make it work. However, in the Lord's time, I received a revelation that Christ lived in me. Now I can say, I died on the cross in Christ, and there is no more I can do through my own self-effort to make things work.

I think we have all had someone come to us and tell us we need to carry our cross. I run into many people who tell me the cross they have to bear is too heavy. When I hear that, I tend to draw back because under grace God never allows more to be put on us than we can bear. I think an ironic aspect of Jesus telling people to pick up their cross is that when the time came for Him to carry His cross, He was so heavily laden with our sin and suffering in His body that He was unable to do so Himself. Simon the Cyrene had to be enlisted to carry the cross of Jesus (Matt. 27:32).

I recall a time in a large revival meeting when a lady in the crowd came to the front and was praying for the people who had come forward for help. As she prayed, many of the people received blessings. After the service, I walked over to her and told her how I appreciated her help, and encouraged her to come forward and pray for people as the week progressed. She looked at me pitifully and said, "Oh, brother, I don't think I can come back to the meetings as I have such a heavy cross to bear." I asked her what she meant by having a "heavy cross." She replied, "I married an unsaved man, and he will not let me go to meetings when I want to." I looked at the woman and said, "Lady, that is not a cross, that is a mistake you made and now you have to live with it."

On another occasion, I recall a lady coming to me at a meeting. She had heard me speaking about the Cross, and she told me she had a very heavy cross to bear. She told me this story. Forty years ago, when she was 18 years old, her mother came down with Alzheimer's disease. Her mother was still living, but her father had died two years earlier. There were no other children in the family, nor were there any other close relatives and very little money. She was the only person who could take care of her mother. Occasionally, someone would relieve her for a day, but she had been providing care for her mother for 40 years. She said she never had a life of her own. She could never date, had never married, and will never have children of her own. She looked at me and said, "I've had a heavy cross, don't you think?" Although my heart went out to her, I told her that there was no doubt she was describing a rough life, but the load she was carrying was not her cross, but her ministry! Her mother's care was her ministry of love.

Another aspect of the Cross that is often misunderstood is that Calvary is the last altar. The word *altar* is rarely used in the New Testament, and when it is, it often refers back to the Old Testament. The reason for this, I believe, is that there is no New Testament altar for born-again believers after the Cross of Calvary. Many Christians are busy building physical and spiritual altars to the Lord, but that all ended with Calvary's Cross. The Cross of Calvary is the last altar recognized by God, where the ultimate and last sacrifice took place.

The Apostle Paul's message is that in this world we are going to experience hurt, pain, and even death someday. His message is that we are not body people and we don't understand and relate to God based upon what happens in our bodies. We don't relate to God with our bodies, but rather through spirit (1 Cor. 6:17).

Jesus of Nazareth did not mention the Cross as a place of salvation because He primarily preached a different message to Israel. Before the Cross, the nation of Israel could only be saved by the gospel of circumcision, requiring repentance and water baptism. There was no Cross of salvation until Jesus died on the Cross. Crucifixion was not considered a place of salvation prior to Calvary.

When Peter preached his great sermon on the Day of Pentecost, he was still preaching the kingdom message (gospel of circumcision). He condemned the Jews for crucifying Jesus. That is not the gospel for the new-creation believer—those who have a new life in Christ—nor is it salvation through the shed blood of Jesus Christ. Many ministers bring hungry hearts to Christ quoting Peter's sermon text. *"Then Peter said unto them, Repent, and be baptized every one of you in the name of Jesus Christ for the remission of sins, and ye shall receive the gift of the Holy Ghost"* (Acts 2:38). Peter never mentioned the Cross. On the Day of Pentecost, 3,000 were saved, and later another 5,000 were saved. They were all born again, but I don't believe any of them knew what it meant. They did not know they were saved by the Cross. They did not know Christ was in them by the birthing, by the Father placing His incorruptible seed, Christ, in them (1 Peter 1:23). They did not know what it meant to be "in Christ."

Total Salvation

The first in-Christ message occurs at Gethsemane. When Jesus knelt in Gethsemane and drank the cup, that cup contained all the sin of the world. It included every person who had lived up until that time and everyone who will ever live. When Jesus drank the cup, all sin, finally and ultimately, was in that cup. The absolution of sin by slain animals in the Old Testament was only temporary and had to be repeated each year. Later, when Paul wrote, *"When it pleased God ... to reveal His Son in me"* (Gal. 1:15–16), he was describing what happened on one side of the Cross, after

Calvary. On the other side of the Cross, in Gethsemane, every human being with their sin, shame, and suf-suffering, was poured into Christ's body.

A Sinless Jesus

Have you ever wondered why Jesus was given a prepared body? In Hebrews 10:5, the Scripture states, *"A body hast thou prepared me."* Jesus had a body without sin. He would never pay the price for His own sin, as He did not have any. Ultimate love demanded that He pay the price for others, never for Himself. His death was not because of His failure but because of our failure. So a sinless body was prepared for Christ. *"For he hath made him to be sin for us, who knew no sin; that we might be made the righteousness of God in him"* (2 Cor. 5:21). In Gethsemane, our sin, our suffering, our disease, and our death were poured into His body. Every malady that came from the curse of sin was poured into His body. Retribution was made for everything that separated us from the Father.

The First Body of Christ

Mary produced a very special body for Jesus. When God put His seed in that body, God the Son lived there in a sinless condition. Jesus could have committed sin, but He never did. This fact is important because when Jesus drank the cup in Gethsemane His body was the means of devouring and eliminating every sin that was put into that body. That was the only way sin could be taken care of. The Old Testament said sin is death (Gen. 2:17).

Many believers live their entire lives without knowing they were in Christ in Gethsemane. They don't know they were in Christ when He was nailed to the cross. The Scriptures say Christ died for our sins, but that is not the message the Apostle Paul brings to us. The Apostle Paul told us it is our death that took place on the cross. We died on the cross. I must die somewhere, but I cannot die for myself and be saved. However, Christ did not just die for me, He died as me! Every time you look at a cross, don't just see Jesus on it, see yourself on it.

Know No Man after the Flesh

In 2 Corinthians 5:16, Paul made an outlandish statement by saying we no longer know Jesus in the flesh: *"Wherefore henceforth know we no man after the flesh: yea, though we have known Christ after the flesh, yet now henceforth know we him no more."* Paul never mentioned Jesus in the flesh. He did not mention His virgin birth, His miracles, the healings, raising people from the dead, or a sermon Jesus preached. Paul did not mention Jesus in the flesh because that part of Jesus' life has nothing to do with who we are as new-creation believers! What did Paul mention about Jesus of Nazareth? Paul wrote about Jesus' death, burial, resurrection, and ascension. Paul focused on these events in the life of Jesus of Nazareth because they are the times you and I are in Christ. It makes sense that Paul said we are not to know Jesus outside of our death, burial, resurrection, and ascension in Him. We are not followers of Jesus of Nazareth; we are birthed children of God, which is an entirely different understanding. We need to know how we came into Christ, and this knowledge is what Paul emphasized.

Paul's Understanding of the Cross

It is my belief that when Paul saw that Christ was in him, his entire ministry and understanding concerning the Cross was radically changed. The Apostle Paul realized that if the plan of God was that another was to live in us, then our entire existence depended upon this other one. Paul's message of grace is that nothing depends upon the human being except to believe on the Lord Jesus Christ. Everything God has to do with a person depends upon Christ who lives in that person.

Religion depends on you living the Christian life, you being good, you taking up a certain doctrine, you receiving someone's baptism, you becoming a member of a church and you doing things according to that church's rules. But when God puts Christ in a human being, from that moment on He never depends on that human being again. Why would God put Jesus in me and then turn around and depend upon me? That would be foolish, wouldn't it? What in the world could I add to Christ? What can I add to the Cross? What can I add to the work of the Holy Spirit? What can I add to God's stature? Nothing!   FAITH + NOTHING

God had already illustrated in 4,300 years of the Old Testament that man never could please Him. Now God's plan is to birth His own. They will be His children because He puts a part of Himself, part of the Godhead—God, the Son—in them. Now He depends on the one within, and God can now have the children He wanted. That is what 1 Corinthians 12:13 says, *"For by one Spirit* [the Holy Spirit] *are we all baptized into one body* [one person, Christ]. *"* We were put into Christ; we are in Christ, and Christ is in us.

Our Death

Romans 6:3–4, states, *"Know ye not, that so many of us as were baptized into Jesus Christ were baptized into his death? Therefore we are buried with him by baptism into death."* This Scripture is not talking about water baptism! It is talking about the moment you were born again and baptized into the Body of Christ (1 Cor. 12:13).

> *Therefore we are buried with him by baptism into death: that like as Christ was raised up from the dead by the glory of the Father, even so we also should walk in newness of life. For if we have been planted together in the likeness of*

his death, we shall be also in the likeness of his resurrection. (Rom. 6:4–5)

In these verses you need to circle the word *with*. There is nothing that can separate you from Jesus Christ, not your sin, not your shame, not your shortcomings. Aside from Christ, you are nothing. All sinners were in His body at the Cross. The meanest, most vile, most wicked, most ungodly individual who ever lived is dead in Christ at the Cross. Every person who has ever walked the face of this earth is dead in Christ to sin. However, if they don't believe on the Lord Jesus Christ, they are going to hell. *"For God so loved the world, that he gave his only begotten Son, that whosoever believeth in him should not perish, but have everlasting life"* (John 3:16).

There is not an ungodly person in your neighborhood, in your family, or on the job who is not dead in Christ. That means their sin is covered. It means sinners don't have to go to hell because of their sin but because they did not believe on the Lord Jesus Christ (John 3:18). God does not set up something special when a person gets saved. Every person who recognizes his or her need of a Savior comes to God on the basis of their death on the cross because they were in Him at Calvary. They are simply receiving something that has already been done on God's part. A big problem with believers is they don't know they are dead in Christ! When believers have a problem with sin, the best thing they can do is to go back to the Cross because that is where God took care of sin.

Paul saw the consequences of Christ in us and us in Christ. The fact is that since you have been re-birthed, you have never had anything happen to you outside of Jesus Christ. God only deals with you on the basis of Jesus Christ and what Christ has done as you. There is no "you" at any point, aside from Christ in you. The Apostle Paul was the first to know that fact. The world would be a lot better off if it would listen to the Apostle Paul because he never veers from this message. That is why he said he is determined to know nothing *"among you, save Jesus Christ, and Him crucified"* (1 Cor. 2:2). When you died on the cross, there was nothing more that could be done. The Cross is a finished work, and all you can do is to believe it!

The "deeper life" people don't know the Cross is a finished work. The idea of self-effort is the shortcoming of the deeper life message. As soon as someone says you need to do this or that to keep your salvation, they have nullified the Cross. The greatest power in my life is the power of the finished work of Christ on the cross.

A woman told me she had such an awful thing in her life that she could not get rid of it. I looked her straight in the eye and said, "Well, you have never been to the Cross. You have never seen your death." The same is true of people who are always trying to die to something—the people who say, *I have to die to my (drinking, overeating, or selfishness, or whatever the shortcoming).* This cannot be so because they are already dead! You cannot die to something to which you are already dead. What you can do is fix it in your mind that you are dead to it.

Most of us have tried all of our lives to become something we already are. You are already dead. This is the reason Paul said, *"Likewise reckon ye also yourselves to be dead indeed unto sin, but alive unto God through Jesus Christ our Lord"* (Rom. 6:11). You are never going to find out who you are until you concentrate on your position in Christ.

Chapter 2
Review Questions

1. How would you define or describe a "kingdom" person?

2. In your own words, describe why the Cross of Calvary is so important to Christianity.

3. What does "taking up your cross daily" mean to you?

4. In this present age, the Church age or the age of grace, what must take place in order for a person to be born again?

5. What does the Scripture, *"For by one Spirit are we all baptized into one body"* (1 Cor. 12:13) mean to you?

6. When all is said and done, what causes people to go to hell?

7. Oftentimes you hear born-again believers talk about "altars" in their lives. What is the one and only altar for the born-again believer?

And straightway he preached Christ in the synagogues, that he is the Son of God. ... Saul increased the more in strength, and confounded the Jews which dwelt at Damascus, proving that this is very Christ. And after that many days were fulfilled, the Jews took counsel to kill him: But their laying await was known of Saul. And they watched the gates day and night to kill him. Then the disciples took him by night, and let him down by the wall in a basket. (Acts 9:20–25)

CHAPTER 3
Paul and the Holy Spirit

Introduction

The Apostle Paul cannot be compared to Christ as Christ is God and Paul is a mere mortal man. An important thing about the Apostle Paul, however, is that God gave him the truth that concerns us today. This is why Paul said, *"Be ye followers of me, even as I also am of Christ"* (1 Cor. 11:1) Paul knew that the message of the Dispensation of Grace—which Christ committed to him through revelation—differed from the teachings of Jesus of Nazareth to Israel (See Gal. 1:12; 1 Cor. 9:17; Eph. 3:2; and Col. 1:25). In this Dispensation of Grace, we are to follow Paul's teaching of Christ in the inner man rather than focus on the earthly ministry of Jesus of Nazareth. Paul is the key to understanding what belongs to us in the message of grace. This understanding is generally unknown to most in the Church.

For the most part, we read the Bible and mix it together as one message. The problem with this approach is that the way God deals with us today, in the message of grace, is different from the way He dealt with people under the law, in the time from Moses to the Day of Pentecost. By the same token, when He dealt with people under the law, it was different from the way He worked with people in previous time periods or dispensations. Whatever terminology you want to use really doesn't matter, but you must recognize that, throughout history, God has done several different things in the Scriptures, and we cannot mix these together. Believers and theologians are guilty of taking verses from the law period and applying them to the

Church today. While certain applications may be edifying, God does not speak to Gentiles through the law. The error occurs when they choose a verse in which God is not talking to us. Conversely, when God says something directly to those of us who are born-again believers, we need to listen to it clearly. The only place in the Bible where God speaks directly to us is in Paul's epistles; therefore, I place emphasis on the Apostle Paul. Never in the Scriptures before Paul was it revealed that God would place His Son in a creature and place that creature in His Son. Until Paul had his revelation of the mystery in the Arabian Desert, the final gospel could not be completed.

Paul becomes central to our understanding because he ties the entire plan of God together based upon his revelation. If you know Christ lives in you (another person is in you), and that the essence of this understanding is that you no longer live, then everything you believe and everything you touch is based upon this knowledge. For the most part, that has not happened in Christianity. Everything Paul taught was based on *"Christ in you, the hope of glory"* (Col. 1:27).

To illustrate the power of this understanding, let us assume that through a great scientific miracle I could live in your body so that when you did anything it would be my strength and it would be your mouth speaking my words. This understanding would change everything about you. It would change the way you eat, the way you walk, the way you work, the way you live—everything about you would be different from that viewpoint. You would not continue living as you used to do. It was the same with the Apostle Paul when he had the revelation that Christ lived in him. This becomes very evident when you read the third chapter of Philippians, where he listed everything that was in his life, his past and present, and said, *"I count all things but loss for the excellency of the knowledge of Christ*

Jesus my Lord" (Phil. 3:8). Paul is describing the tremendous change that occurred in his life because of the knowledge he had received. When it became clear to me that he did not preach the same gospel Peter preached, and I saw that Paul called the gospel he preached "my gospel" (Rom. 2:16; 16:25; and 2 Tim. 2:8), the same thing happened in my life.

The Trinity

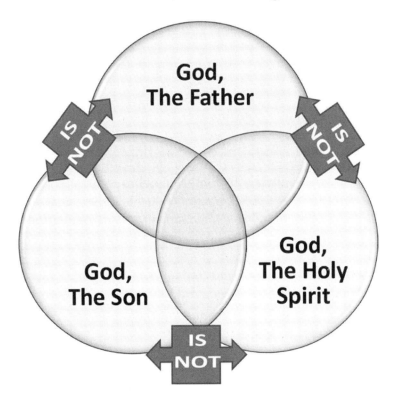

Figure 1

The Holy Spirit and the Trinity
I want to lay a foundation for your understanding of the work of the Holy Spirit (See figure 1.). The first university I attended was Baylor University,

which was the largest Baptist institution in the world. I remember one day we had a class on the Trinity. Baptists are very strong on the doctrine of the Trinity. I recall the teacher drawing a triangle and in the middle of the triangle he wrote the word *God*.

The Bible is very clear that there is but one God (Isa. 43:10; 44:6, 8; 45:5; 46:9; and James 2:19). Each of the three points of the triangle he labeled as Father, Son, and Holy Spirit. We usually refer to it as three persons in one God. It is just one God, and He has allowed Himself to be manifested in three distinct persons. This truth appears in such Scriptures as Matthew 3:16–17; 28:19; John 15:26; 2 Corinthians 13:14; Ephesians 2:18; 1 Peter 1:2, and 1 John 5:7.

When you look at the triangle, it should tell you that the Father is not the Son, the Son is not the Holy Spirit, and the Holy Spirit is not the Father. At the same time, the Father, the Son, and the Holy Spirit are God.

The Father is shown to be God by such Scriptures as Romans 1:7 and 1 Corinthians 8:6. Christ is shown to be God in John 1:1, 14, and 5:17–18. The Holy Spirit is referred to as God in Acts 5:3–4. These distinctions are very important for you to understand; many Christians don't see or believe this.

The Ministry of the Holy Spirit

To further build on this foundation for understanding the work of the Holy Spirit, you must recognize this central truth: the Holy Spirit's ministry is to teach us Christ. His ministry becomes clear when you read the message Jesus gave in John chapters 14, 15, and 16. I stress this point because that is the only place in the Scriptures where Jesus, God the Son, told us what the Holy Spirit would do. In these chapters, He described the Holy Spirit being active in the mind, or as we often refer to it, the soul (the mind, will, and emotions). He talked about sinners being convicted.

Conviction is a mind-thing because the mind is where you make decisions. The Holy Spirit's teaching renews our minds.

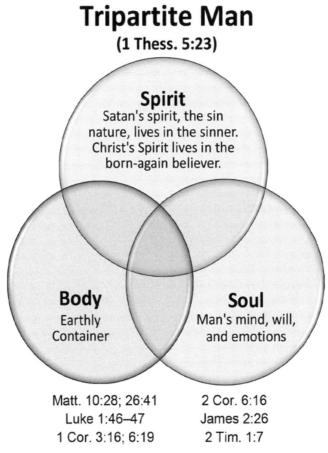

Tripartite Man
(1 Thess. 5:23)

Spirit
Satan's spirit, the sin nature, lives in the sinner. Christ's Spirit lives in the born-again believer.

Body
Earthly Container

Soul
Man's mind, will, and emotions

Matt. 10:28; 26:41
Luke 1:46–47
1 Cor. 3:16; 6:19

2 Cor. 6:16
James 2:26
2 Tim. 1:7

Figure 2

Tripartite Man

    I emphasize this point about the ministry of the Holy Spirit taking place in your soul/mind because it is important to distinguish what happens there from what takes place in your spirit. We are composed of body, soul, and spirit (1 Thess. 5:23, see figure 2).

When we were born again, Jesus was joined to our spirit. The Scripture states, *"But he that is joined unto the Lord is one spirit"* (1 Cor. 6:17). Notice Paul did not say he was joined to the Spirit of the Lord. Christians have a fuzzy notion that the Spirit of Christ and the Holy Spirit are one and the same. To me, that is one of the greatest errors in Christianity. Paul never used that terminology. It is the same precision Paul used when he did not say, *My spirit is crucified with Christ.* He said, *"I am crucified with Christ"* (Gal. 2:20). The difference is that he did not remove the personhood (the "I") out of the statement! I am trying to make it clear that when the Apostle Paul spoke of Christ in the believer he was not talking about the Holy Spirit.

Modern Christianity teaches that when you accept Jesus as your Savior, the Holy Spirit comes in and He lives His life through you. This view is contrary to the Word of God, a commingling of Scriptures, because it does not reflect a careful reading of Paul's epistles. I have Christ as a person in me so that I can grow in His grace. He will come through me as I am. He has been made unto me wisdom, righteousness, sanctification, and redemption (1 Cor. 1:30). When a person is born again, Christ is joined to their spirit. It is Christ in our spirit.

When the Scripture talks about being filled with the Holy Spirit (Acts 2:4; 4:8, 31; 9:17; 13:9), or being baptized into the Holy Spirit (Acts 1:5; 11:16), what does it mean? These Scriptures are talking about the Holy Spirit coming to do the main mission He is commissioned to do: to glorify Christ. Where will He do it? He will do it in our souls/minds. His purpose is to live in me as my Teacher and work in my understanding.

The work of the Holy Spirit is in our souls/minds (1 Cor. 2:9–14). Jesus told His disciples:

Howbeit when he, the Spirit of truth [the Holy Spirit], *is come, he will guide you into all truth: for he shall not speak of himself; but whatsoever he shall hear, that shall he speak: and he will show you things to come. He shall glorify me: for he shall receive of mine, and shall show it unto you.* (John 16:13–14)

The speaking is done in our minds. For believers to come to the knowledge that Christ lives in them is the work designated to the Holy Spirit. Paul used statements such as Ephesians 4:20, *"But ye have not so learned Christ."* We learn Christ through our minds. That is the work of the Holy Spirit. The Holy Spirit is not to take the place of Christ, but to teach us Christ. Jesus said in John 14:26, *"The Comforter, which is the Holy Ghost, whom the Father will send in my name, he shall teach you all things, and bring all things to your remembrance."* The purpose of the Holy Spirit is to teach us.

Multitudes of believers misuse the Holy Spirit in them for something other than the Scriptures teach. They will not let Him do what He is supposed to do. Many churches don't want you to be taught by the Spirit. They throw words around about being led by the Spirit, but they will not let you be taught by the Spirit because you will not need them and their personal ministries. Instead, to put you in bondage to their ministries, they use such Scriptures as, *"How shall they hear without a preacher?"* (Rom. 10:14), which refers to the unsaved. The Spirit does not teach the unsaved. A preacher can deliver the message while the Spirit convicts the sinner. (Note John 16:8–11 talks of how the Holy Spirit would deal with *"the world,"* meaning the unsaved.) This is not the same as dealing with birthed sons of the Father. I am talking about people who are at a different level, those who are growing in the deeper things of God, taught by the Holy Spirit. Now, I don't mean you can't learn from others, but if you don't have the Holy Spirit revealing the Christ who is in you, you will never come to be who you are supposed to be. Christianity is Christ living in you, but more important than living in you is Christ living through you. It is easy to say, *I have Christ in me.* But what the Holy Spirit does is bring Christ out through me.

Is the Holy Spirit *upon* Men or *in* Them?

In the Old Testament, before the days of Jesus of Nazareth, the Holy Spirit came upon men. After the days of Jesus of Nazareth, the Holy Spirit was in men. There is no way you can commingle these two things together without being in error. In John 14:17, Jesus said, *"For he* [the Holy Spirit] *dwelleth with you* [before the Day of Pentecost] *and shall be in you* [after the Day of Pentecost]. *"* Throughout the Old Testament, the Holy Spirit moved outside of man. The Holy Spirit is the agent who carries out God's plan. When Jesus was born of Mary, the Holy Spirit came upon Mary, and God had the Holy Spirit place the God-seed in Mary (Luke 1:35).

Remember, there is a distinct delineation between the Father, the Son, and the Holy Spirit. The Son is not the Holy Spirit, although much of Christian theology seems to have made them synonymous. The Son is certainly not the Father, and the Holy Spirit is not the Father. In the Old Testament, the Spirit of the Lord moved upon people. He was not in anyone. The following Scriptures show how the Holy Spirit worked in the Old Testament:

- *"When the spirit rested upon them"* (Num. 11:25, speaking of the seventy elders).
- *"Balaam lifted up his eyes ... and the spirit of God came upon him"* (Num. 24:2).
- *"And the spirit of the Lord came upon him* [Othniel]*"* (Judg. 3:10–11).

- *"The Spirit of God came upon him [Saul] and he prophesied among them"* (1 Sam. 10:10).

- *"The Spirit of the Lord came upon David from that day forward"* (1 Sam. 16:13).

- *"The Spirit of God was upon the messengers of Saul, and they also prophesied"* (1 Sam. 19:20).

- *"The Holy Ghost was upon him* [Simeon]*"* (Luke 2:25).

- *"And there appeared unto them cloven tongues like as of fire, and it sat upon each of them"* (Acts 2:3).

- *"While Peter yet spake these words, the Holy Ghost fell on all them which heard the word"* (Acts 10:44).

- *"And when Paul had laid his hands upon them, the Holy Ghost came on them; and they spake with tongues, and prophesied"* (Acts 19:6).

The significance of these Scriptures is that the Spirit had been with them. He had not been in them, but He came upon them. The work of the Holy Spirit had been outside of man. However, Jesus said the day would come when the Holy Spirit would be in man. Although Luke, in the book of Acts, still speaks of the Spirit coming upon them, the promise of Jesus that the Holy Spirit would be in them took place. The significance is that the Holy Spirit would be constantly revealing Christ in us. The revelation of Christ as your life may be a one-time experience, but every day the Holy Spirit is there to reveal a greater understanding of Christ to you in every circumstance and situation. The Holy Spirit does not take Christ's place in our spirit. He works in the soul/mind.

The Outer Works of the Holy Spirit

Most people are not made believers by the outer works of the Holy Spirit. From the very beginning, when God delivered Israel out of Pharaoh's bondage, He gathered to Himself a chosen people through raising up Moses. Israel was a cantankerous and unbelieving people. No one in the history of the Bible ever had more miracles than Israel had, and no group ever doubted God more than Israel did. All the plagues and curses God sent on Pharaoh caused Israel to want to get out of bondage, yet, there was no genuine change in her heart. Moses raised the rod and opened the Red Sea, and they walked across dry land and saw their enemies swallowed up. Did that make believers out of them? No, it did not! The minute they arrived in the wilderness they wanted to stay there. Stay they did, for 40 years in unbelief, even though Israel had seen these great miracles by the Holy Spirit. All the way through Israel's history she had signs, wonders, and miracles. All the miracles in the wilderness only made Israel want to stay there in unbelief. Even the miracles in Canaan did not make believers out of the people. They still wanted to go back to Egypt.

When God sent His Son, born of a woman and fathered by God, Israel still did not believe. *"He came unto his own, and his own* [Israel] *received him not"* (John 1:11). His own people, to whom He was sent, ended up as part of the accusers who contributed to His death. Miracles never straightened Israel out.

When Jesus began His ministry, He called the disciples and said, *"I send you forth as sheep in the midst of wolves"* (Matt. 10:16). *"Go not into the way of the Gentiles ... But go rather to the lost sheep of the house of Israel, And as ye go, preach, saying, the kingdom of heaven is at hand"* (vv. 5–7). And look at this—He pronounced outer works of the Spirit! *"Heal the sick, cleanse the lepers, raise the dead, cast out devils"* (v.

8). What are all these things? They are outer things that are seen, heard, felt, or touched. God's plan was that the miracles would cause them to accept their Messiah. Yet Israel—who had known that it was God who had opened the Red Sea and had protected them in the wilderness—never had a change of heart. My point is the outer things don't bring a change of heart. They were still taken up with the outer things on the Day of Pentecost when they felt the building shaking, saw cloven tongues of fire, witnessed the speaking in tongues, and saw 3,000 saved. They did not recognize that the Holy Spirit had come as Jesus had said, *"At that day* [Day of Pentecost, when He comes] *ye shall know that I am in my Father, and ye in me, and I in you"* (John 14:20). They did not understand it. All through the book of Acts they were taken up with the outer things.

It is the same in our world today. What we call the great moves of the Spirit are people taken up with the outer things. They love the shouting, the big crowds of people, the singing, the moving of the Spirit, the dancing in the Spirit; they love all of these outer things, but none of this changes their hearts. Their entire focus would change in their search to know God if they were to see Christ as their only life.

There must be a great change in our understanding from the Holy Spirit being *with* people to the Holy Spirit being *in* them. That was left to the Apostle Paul. He was the one to carry out this message.

The Change from the Outer to the Inner

In 1 Corinthians 2:1, Paul begins with a new idea that the outer work of God must become an inner work. *"And I, brethren, when I came to you, came not with excellency of speech or of wisdom, declaring unto you the testimony of God."* Paul said here that he had no sensational flair. He had no great miracles to tell them about. No great stories to tell them. He did not come with excellency of speech or wisdom but declaring what God wants. In verse 2, Paul continued, *"For I determined not to know any thing among you, save Jesus Christ, and Him crucified."* Now that is different!

Someone once said to me, "All you talk about is Christ. Why don't you teach more on secular matters, like how to raise your children, how to control your finances, or how to save your marriage?" My answer was simple but not very gratifying. If we knew Christ as our life, we would have the answer to all these questions. Do you know what makes a good marriage? Two people who know Christ as their life. Do you know how to run a business? By letting Christ be the operator through you. It is not just making Him your partner; it is giving Him the business and you working for Him. There is no sense in giving you four rules on how to set your finances in order when you have Christ in you to be your life. If you were to follow my four rules, and they were contrary to the Christ in you, it would not be worthwhile. If you could suffer the loss of all things, as Paul did, for the excellency of knowing Christ, then you would be headed in the right direction (Phil. 3:8). The true gospel is that we know nothing but Christ as our all and in all.

First Corinthians 2:7 is also an important verse: *"But we speak the wisdom of God in a mystery, even the hidden wisdom, which God ordained before the world unto our glory."* Paul said this work of the Holy Spirit in us, teaching us Christ, is something God intended before the world started. Paul's first attempt to bring the Holy Spirit from the outer to the inner is done in verses 9–10,

> *But as it is written, Eye hath not seen, nor ear heard, neither have entered into the heart of man, the things which God hath prepared for them that love him. But God hath revealed them*

unto us by his Spirit; for the Spirit searcheth all things, yea, the deep things of God.

In my lifetime, I have preached these verses in two different ways. The first way I preached them was on a faith level. I told people, "You have not seen, and you have not heard, and you have not felt the great things God can do because you don't have great faith." But that is not what these verses say at all. They say the deep things of God cannot be seen and cannot be heard and cannot be felt. Then how do you get the deeper things of God? The Spirit must reveal these things! The Holy Spirit is God's agent working in your mind. He brings you the message.

You are never going to see what God can do, hear what God can say, or feel what God can do as a natural man, no matter how much faith you have or try to get. It is only by the Holy Spirit revealing the Christ in you that you can truly know God's work in your life.

Christ Is Love

First Corinthians 13 is often called "the love chapter." Many times, I have tried to explain to people why God put the love chapter in the midst of chapters 12 and 14, which deal with Pentecostalism. These people were exercising all the outer gifts such as tongues and prophecy. In chapter 14, Paul has to talk about how to control these outer gifts. Why would he put this love chapter in there? I used to say it was because all this should be done in love, but I no longer believe that is the whole answer. He put the love chapter in there to bring people from the outer demonstration of the Spirit to the inner relationship with Christ. You may not understand the love chapter unless we make a little change in it. In 1 Corinthians 13, I am going to change the word *charity* to the word *Christ*. I want you to think about the meaning of this passage of Scripture with this change in it.

Though I speak with the tongues of men and of angels, and have not [Christ], *I am become as sounding brass, or a tinkling cymbal.* [Did you ever notice the sounding brass and the tinkling cymbal where Christ is not?] *And though I have the gift of prophecy, and understand all mysteries, and all knowledge; and though I have all faith, so that I could remove mountains, and have not* [Christ], *I am nothing. And though I bestow all my goods to feed the poor, and though I give my body to be burned, and have not* [Christ], *it profiteth me nothing.* [Christ] *suffereth long and is kind;* [Christ] *envieth not;* [Christ] *vaunteth not* [him]*self, is not puffed up, doth not behave* [him]*self unseemly, seeketh not* [his] *own, is not easily provoked, thinketh no evil; rejoiceth not in iniquity, but rejoiceth in the truth; beareth all things, believeth all things, hopeth all things, endureth all things.* [Christ] *never faileth: but whether there be prophecies, they shall fail; whether there be tongues, they shall cease; whether there be knowledge, it shall vanish away. For we know in part, and we prophesy in part.* [Now here comes the key verse:] *But when that which is perfect is come, then that which is in part shall be done away.* (vv. 1–10)

Most non-Pentecostal teachers will say *"that which is in part"* refers to the fact that they did not have the completed Scriptures, but now that we have the whole Bible, they believe, *"that which is in part"* is done away with. I don't believe that is the answer. What is the only perfect thing on this earth? Christ in the believer! *"When that which is perfect is come, then that which is in part shall be done away."* I changed the word *charity* to the word *Christ* because Christ in the believer is all these things.

What is perfect about you and me? Christ in us! First Corinthians 1:30 says, *"But of him are ye in Christ Jesus, who of God is made unto us wisdom, and righteousness, and sanctification, and redemption."* When God looks at me, He sees me as perfect. I am perfect to Him because He sees Christ in me. I am crucified and can no longer live on my own. Yet I still have ways of my own, brought about by my un-renewed mind; and that is where I need the Holy Spirit. The Holy Spirit will constantly turn my mind to the Christ who lives in me so that I can manifest Christ and allow Christ to work out of me. When that which is perfect comes, these outer things fade away. Does that mean all the ministries of the Spirit mentioned in 1 Corinthians 12 and 14 pass away? Not at all. Let's see how this works.

Levels of Understanding

To appreciate this difference, it helps to look at the levels of understanding delineated by Paul in verse 11 of this same chapter 13. *"When I was a child, I spake as a child, I understood as a child, I thought as a child; but when I became a man, I put away childish things."* Here he contrasts our child level of understanding with the man level. This takes us over to 1 John 2:12–14, where we see there are three levels of understanding: the child level, the young man level, and the father level. The man level in 1 Corinthians 13 is the father level in 1 John 2. What did John say the father, or the man level of understanding was? It was one who had *"known him that is from the beginning."* On the father level, you put away childish things, which are the outer things you see, hear, and feel. Your level of understanding at the father level knows from the beginning. What does John mean by that? I believe he means that our gospel is based on what took place before the foundation of the world, the beginning. Remember, the beginning of our grace gospel is before the world was created (Eph. 1:4). First Corinthians

13:12 states, *"For now we see through a glass, darkly; but then face to face: now I know in part; but then shall I know even as also I am known."* We must ask the question, *When will I know who I am?* The answer, I believe, is when Christ is revealed in me. I will be known as a child of God, an offspring of God, a birthed son of God. How do I come to that conclusion? *"But we all, with open face beholding as in a glass the glory of the Lord, are changed into the same image from glory to glory, even as by the Spirit of the Lord"* (2 Cor. 3:18). I hold up the mirror, the Scriptures; and I see His face in the mirror, and it changes me. I see His face, and by looking upon Him, I am changed from glory to glory. I see it darkly at first, but the time comes when Christ is revealed in me, and I know perfectly that Christ lives in me.

The Five-fold Ministry

One of the great controversies I face everywhere I go is people asking, "Do you folks believe in the five-fold ministry of Ephesians 4:11?" My answer to them is that we do believe in the five-fold ministry. Then they usually ask, "How many apostles are in the Christ-life?" I say, "Several hundred. We make everyone in the Christ-life an apostle. Everyone who comes into the Christ-life is made a prophet." "Can this be so?" they usually ask. I reply, "Christ lives in them, and Christ is the apostle; Christ is the prophet. If the Holy Spirit so elects, even the least of our believers can be an apostle, and do His work, or do the work of a prophet, a pastor, a teacher, and an evangelist because we understand that Christ is the only one who lives, so He has to be everything. That means we all have these ministries because we have Christ in us."

Looking at the beginning of Ephesians 4:8–12, we see it was Christ who set up the New Testament Church in this manner. Why did He set up apostles, prophets, pastors, teachers, and evangelists? Jesus knew the early Church would not grasp the idea of Christ in you right away. Paul had not yet received the revelation; and until he did, it could not be preached. Paul's revelation came about 13 years after the Day of Pentecost. Therefore, the early Church went through a period of time focusing on the outer things and believers did not know Christ lived in them. They were all born again on the Day of Pentecost with Christ in them, but they did not know it. They were still distracted with the outer things.

When Paul received his revelation that Christ lived in the believer, there was a great difference between his understanding and Peter's understanding. Peter was still looking for the outer things to establish the earthly kingdom. Paul was interested in knowing what it meant to have Christ in us and how that knowledge would affect the new Body of Christ on earth, the Church. We have only scratched the surface of this great truth of Christ in you and what that means. There is no end to it! When we come to the knowledge of Christ in us as our only life, these other "self-ministries" become secondary.

The Holy Spirit Is Not Christ

Separating the Holy Spirit from Christ is an endless task in today's world. Religion seems to be intent on making the Holy Spirit and Christ the same. Most books by theologians say the same thing. They say, *Christ saves me, and Christ is our life;* but then they say, *The Holy Spirit comes into me and is the only Spirit in me.* If Paul was clear on anything in his message it was that he no longer lived and the life he lived was Christ (Gal. 2:20), not the Holy Spirit. The Holy Spirit helps me by teaching me the Christ who is in me, but He is not my life. My life is Christ!

Remember this too: when the incorruptible seed, Christ the Word, was put in you (1 Peter 1:23), it was total. There is no more seed to come into you. When you become a partaker of God's divine nature (2 Peter 1:4), you are total and complete in spirit. You are not growing anymore in the spirit. The only place you can grow is in knowledge, in your soul/mind, and that is where the Holy Spirit works. The fullness of Christ is in you, but too often your problem is that you don't know it. How are you going to come to know it? By being taught by the Holy Spirit in your mind.

The following facts should be kept in mind when we think about the Holy Spirit:

1. The misuse of the Holy Spirit is the reason believers don't know they are in Christ. If they never had a book, a teacher, or a tape on the subject, they could still learn that they are in Christ if they would listen to the Holy Spirit. His mission is to speak only of Christ.

2. The misuse of the Holy Spirit has attributed gifts to men rather than Christ being their life and Christ being the gifted one. Some preacher may come to a city and advertise stating, "I am God's man for the hour." This is not correct. Christ is God's man in that preacher because that preacher no longer lives. Christ lives through him. When we don't have the Holy Spirit revealing Christ to us, men claim to have the gifts rather than Christ being the life.

3. Denying the Holy Spirit His place as Teacher perpetuates law-religion. If the Holy Spirit is not teaching believers, then they are being taught by the five-fold ministers. Often, these ministers teach what to do and how to do it rather than who is your life. We all know that the five-fold ministries can fail. We would not want to stake our relationship with God on what man says. We need to let the Holy Spirit be the one who teaches us the Christ who is in us.

4. I know of no Scripture that says the Holy Spirit takes the place of Christ in the believer.

5. The Holy Spirit is not the Savior. He is not the crucified one. He is not the buried one. He is not the resurrected one, and He is not the ascended one.

6. Jesus taught that the Holy Spirit was a teacher. *"But ye shall receive power, after that the Holy Ghost is come upon you"* (Acts 1:8). Why is the word *after* in this verse? In this case, it means after He has taught, and after He has trained, then you will have the real power. The real power of a believer is in knowing the Christ who is within.

7. The Holy Spirit is not the one who is joined to our spirit. *"He that is joined unto the Lord is one spirit"* (1 Cor. 6:17). He operates solely in our soulish area, our soul/mind. It is Christ, the Lord, who is joined to our spirit.

8. The Holy Spirit is not life. The life is in the Son. *"He that hath the Son hath life; and he that hath not the Son of God hath not life"* (1 John 5:12).

9. If the Holy Spirit is life, or the one who gives us His life, our relationship with Christ will always be elusive. We have always taught people that they need to be filled with the Holy Spirit. That very statement suggests that you were filled, but now you are empty! Now you need to be filled with the Holy Spirit again. That understanding implies that I am saved sometimes and not saved other times. If it depends on me being filled with the Holy Spirit to be saved, then my salvation is never secure. My salvation is not based on the Holy Spirit.

My salvation is based on a knowing. *"For I know whom I have believed"* (2 Tim. 1:12).

10. The work of the Holy Spirit brings us to our need of salvation (John 16:8), and He also places us in Christ (Eph. 1:13). However, salvation is determined by Christ in you. First Corinthians 12:13 states, *"For by one Spirit* [the Holy Spirit] *are we all baptized into one body* [Christ]. *"* The Holy Spirit brings us to our need of salvation; and He places us in Christ; but He is not Christ. He is not the life. The life is in the Son.

11. The Holy Spirit is not the incorruptible seed (1 Peter 1:23); neither is He the divine nature that was placed in you (2 Peter 1:4).

12. The Scriptures say we are in Christ. They never say we are in the Holy Spirit.

Conclusion

It has been my desire in writing this chapter that you may understand the difference between the indwelling of the Holy Spirit, and the indwelling of Christ. Each is God, and each has a special ministry of vital importance in our understanding of who and what we are as spirit-beings. However, the Holy Spirit and Christ are not one and the same person. The Holy Spirit is the revealer of Christ in us, but He is never Christ. It is Christ in us who is our only hope of glory (Col. 1:27), and our all in all (Eph. 1:23).

Chapter 3
Review Questions

1. In your own words, explain why you think it is important to focus on the epistles written by the Apostle Paul.

2. What is the primary ministry of the Holy Spirit?

3. Describe the difference in the ways in which the Holy Spirit worked prior to the Day of Pentecost and after the Day of Pentecost.

4. How important are signs, wonders, and miracles to you and your belief system?

5. In 1 Corinthians 13:10, the following words appear. *"But when that which is perfect is come, then that which is in part shall be done away."* What is the "perfect" that is to come, and when will it come?

6. Why did the people who were born again on the Day of Pentecost not understand that Christ was now in them?

And there came thither certain Jews from Antioch and Iconium, who persuaded the people, and, having stoned Paul, drew him out of the city, supposing he had been dead. Howbeit, as the disciples stood round about him, he rose up, and came into the city: and the next day he departed with Barnabas to Derbe. (Acts 14:19–20)

CHAPTER 4

Paul and the C & S Gang
(Circumstances & Situations)

Introduction

The burden of bringing the knowledge of a new gospel that encompassed the whole of the Scriptures and the entire plan of God was placed on one man, Paul. If we don't know and understand what God said and did through the Apostle Paul, we miss what God is doing today. Paul is the key to the revelation of God's plan. He is not the heart of God's plan because that is Christ. The Apostle Paul in no way becomes Christ, or becomes a god, or takes the place of Christ; nevertheless, he does become the final voice for Christ because the final gospel is given to him by Jesus Christ, Himself (Gal. 1:11–12). Just as the Lord called the 12 apostles and gave them a gospel for Israel (the message we now call the kingdom message), God strategically called Paul to bring the gospel of the mystery, the gospel of grace.

God Working through Faith

Prior to the Apostle Paul, the only way God worked with humanity was in the area of whether or not the human had enough faith. That is what 4,300 years of the Bible is about, all the way from Adam to Jesus of Nazareth. If Adam had faith in what God said, he would not have gotten into trouble. Abraham, Noah, Daniel, and David were victorious men because of their faith. Their faith worked in the outer things. David went out and removed Goliath. When Daniel was put in the lion's den, God shut the lion's mouth. When a whale swallowed Jonah, God took care of him. It was always God coming on the scene from the outside to help. The idea established in the Scriptures prior to Paul was that if you have trouble, God will take care of it from the outside.

When God put Christ in the believer, it resulted in a radical change in the way God worked with people. The Apostle Paul was the first to see that there was a new gospel, not based on the idea that God will take away your troubles if you have enough faith, but a gospel that says Christ in you is your hope of glory! All your life, you were probably taught that God would solve your problems and take care of your needs in an outer form, if you would just trust Him. Now God depends on Christ in you, not on your faith getting God to do a work outwardly. Grace is a different gospel. The Apostle Paul was the first to teach that difference. Unfortunately, great numbers of people in Christianity have never seen this difference between God taking away all our problems by our own efforts of faith and God trusting Christ who is in us to overcome everything.

Did you ever wonder why God doesn't do the signs, wonders, and miracles that He did in the Old Testament and in the first few years of the early Church? There were signs, wonders, and miracles because God wanted Israel to accept her Messiah. If you watch Christian television and the charismatic preachers of today, you will hear them say the trouble is believers don't have enough faith and if we really want to make our faith work we need to send them an offering. Sending an offering to exercise faith is an extension of doer religion. They preach that we are going to have a great revival in the future, greater than we have ever seen in the past. I don't believe that because these preachers have missed what the Scriptures indicate to me.

In the book of Acts, God moved from doing these great outer things to placing Christ in us. If you miss the in-Christ message, you miss what God is doing today. We are now rebirthed with Christ in us. We are safe in Christ and cannot be any better off than we are as we wait for our day of emancipation from this body of flesh. We have a different gospel. Most of us were not taught this different gospel. We were not taught that a change had taken place. We were not taught how God had used Paul's revelation to move us into a whole new understanding and gospel. These facts make Paul's call and message very strategic.

In Acts 9:15 we have the calling of Paul, *"But the Lord said unto him* [Ananias]*, Go thy way: for he* [Paul] *is a chosen vessel unto me, to bear my name before the Gentiles, and kings, and the children of Israel."* Look at verse 16, *"For I will shew him how great things he must suffer for my name's sake."* Think about what is said here for a moment. Paul had been knocked down, struck blind, and Christ had hollered out of heaven at him to tell him that he had been called to suffer for God. This is a specific call for Paul to suffer for God. Most likely, you are reading this book because you have been through troubles and trials in your life and are looking for an understanding of how and why these come about. You have been through enough heartache in life to know that God does not remove everything in your circumstances and situations. You did not quit; you did not leave God, and God did not leave you, but you did suffer. To go on with the Lord you suffered, and the longer you serve God, the more He is going to bring circumstances and situations into your life.

In 2 Timothy 4:5 the Apostle Paul states, *"But watch thou in all things, endure afflictions."* Nowhere in the Old Testament was a prophet or a servant of God told to endure affliction. They were told to put their faith in God and He would deliver them.

Someone came to me and asked, "Why do most charismatic preachers preach from the Old Testament?" I believe it is because the message of the Old Testament is to put your faith in God and you will be delivered. That Old Testament message is not New Testament, and it is not grace. Grace is certainly not the gospel being preached to us today because people don't want to endure affliction. In 2 Timothy 4:5–7, Paul went on to say, *"Do the work of an evangelist, make full proof of thy ministry. For I am now ready to be offered and the time of my departure is at hand. I have fought a good fight, I have finished my course, I have kept the faith."* There it is in a nutshell. God called me to suffer, and I have done it. *"Henceforth there is laid up for me a crown of righteousness, which the Lord, the righteous judge, shall give me at that day: and not to me only, but unto all them also that love his appearing"* (v. 8). I find it interesting that he said it like that. Do you know what thought comes to most of our minds when we hurt in life? *I would like to go to be with the Lord. I would just like to go see Him.*

In the Christ-life, there are two lessons I think are imperative to this understanding of the radical change from God being outer to Christ being in us. The first is the schoolhouse, and the second is converging powers. The schoolhouse message is where we see that the world is our schoolhouse. This lesson states that all things were created by and for Christ (Col. 1:16). Why are things in this world for Christ? Their purpose is to teach us Christ. Paul said, *"For I determined not to know any thing among you, save Jesus Christ, and him crucified"* (1 Cor. 2:2). That means the only important thing in our lives in this world is Jesus Christ. All you need to know is Jesus Christ in you, nothing else.

The schoolhouse is the world where we are trained. Ever since we were born again, we have been in training to live in the Father's house. We were not born again to live on this earth. The earth does not fit the born-again. The earth fits Israel. Israel is a created people who will not be born again until she accepts her Messiah. Many people hate Israel because she is made to live on this earth and to prosper. You can put an Israelite in a hard place, and they will do just fine. You and I were not made for this earth. We were made to live in the Father's house. We have been rebirthed and have the nature of God within us (2 Peter 1:4); consequently, we don't fit on this earth.

The Apostle Paul saw a thing I call "converging powers." God's purpose for the human being on this earth is that through our circumstances and situations ("the C & S gang"), we would come to know Christ. Through our C & S, we would come to know about this life that is in us. Most people who are born again don't understand Christ is in them to this day. Why doesn't God straighten out our lives? God does not make our lives a velvet walk, or a flower cloud of ease because He wants us to know this Christ who is in us.

One of the big C & S in our lives is marriage. God also works through our employment. He works through finances. He works through our children. He works through religion and our health. I could make an endless list. God uses C & S to push us to Christ. What is marriage? It is a converging power. What is it doing? It is pushing us to Christ.

Someone is always telling me they don't like their job. Until God gives you another one, stick with what you have been given. It is pushing you to Christ. Always remember, if you were not on that job as a Christian, would there be anyone in that place representing Christ as you do? Your job is a converging power! God keeps the pressure on us because we don't know this Jesus who lives in us. Many of you are reading this book today because of the circumstances and situations of life. Those converging powers are pushing you to Christ. Only the Apostle Paul understood this.

The Apostle Paul has a gospel that helps us to understand circumstances and situations. Prior to Paul, all these problems were solved by faith. After the Apostle Paul, we no longer sit around and wait for God to pour out His Spirit and give us a great miracle. Now we have a gospel that says Christ lives in us and He will never leave us nor forsake us (Heb. 13:5). So what is our problem? We have to learn Him! We don't know how to live with Christ in us. It is a whole lot easier to forget Christ in us and pray for God to give us a miracle. When you are doing something on your own, you will probably feel better about it, but you are ignoring the Christ in you. The new gospel is *"Christ in you, the hope of glory"* (Col. 1:27). God gets our attention about this new gospel and teaches us the Christ who is within by using circumstances and situations of this life!

Paul's Awful Lists
This topic is radically different from anything else that has been taught in the Scriptures. I have studied Paul's five awful lists and discovered that they are actually blessings. I call them awful because when you look at them separated from the context of the Scriptures, they are really awful things that happened to Paul. These lists are very important to our spiritual growth and understanding. I chose to write about these lists here because I want you to see and know these Scriptures exist.

In the first list, in Romans 8:35–39, Paul tells us nothing can separate us from Jesus Christ. The gospel of grace says Christ is birthed in us and nothing can separate us from Him. The birthing is key! Most Christians (I often say at least 90 percent) don't understand the birthing. Religion has withheld this knowledge from them in preference to the kingdom message, which focuses on what we do rather than who we are. I know people who really get upset when I use the word *birthing*. When I use it, they think I am weird, but I am talking about being born again. A birthing took place. God birthed in me His dear Son. We have ample Scripture for that (John 3, 1 Peter 1:23; 2 Peter 1:4); but when you state it plainly, it scares some people. As we read Romans 8:35, we see Paul lists the real trials of life. *"Who shall separate us from the love of Christ? Shall tribulation, or distress, or persecution, or famine, or nakedness, or peril, or sword?"* Can you think of anything that can separate you from Jesus Christ? I could, when I preached the law! I said nothing could separate you from Christ except yourself. As law preachers, we said the Bible tells us we are all in God's hands until we jump out of them. This verse tells us, however, that nothing can separate us from the love of God in Christ Jesus! Nothing that happens to you can separate you from Him. The outer gospel—which says God must come and do things for us—gives us a certain feeling. For example, when you get a healing or a miracle or God answers your prayer, you feel real good, and you might think, *God is with me; God is for me, and God is taking care of me.* Also, you could say, *He heard my prayer. Look at what He did. I am just full of praise and thanksgiving.* But Paul said his gospel is different because there is nothing that can separate you from Christ. Whether God does something or not, you cannot be separated from Him.

Continuing on to verse 36 in Romans 8, it says, *"As it is written, For thy sake we are killed all the day long; we are counted as sheep for the slaughter."* Now that is something we did not know! No one ever told us we are counted as sheep headed for the slaughter when we walked down an aisle to get saved, knelt at an altar, gave our heart to God, or whatever it was we did. Most of us heard that life was going to work out fine if we gave our heart to God. Everything was going to go smoothly. God was going to bless our family, our work, and our children. That was not the exact truth. Why would the Scriptures give us this verse when coming to God ought to be a blessing? The Old Testament speaks of God blessing the people, but that is another gospel based on God doing something based on someone's faith. The gospel from Paul is Christ in the believer, the gift of God. We are counted as sheep led to the slaughter because it hurts to have all those converging powers working in our lives, pushing us to Christ. Most Christians would rather have God take these converging powers away. We would rather have God heal our bodies than bear the burden of poor health. We would rather have God save our children and get them ready for heaven than deal with their problems. We would like Him to do something for us. Instead, He put Christ in us. We need to learn Christ in us and allow Him to handle these things, not learn how we should live life. It is Christ living the life in and through us, a reality that is important to understand.

Romans 8:37 says, *"Nay, in all these things we are more than conquerors through him that loved us."* Do you understand that the person who is able to trust the Christ in him is a conqueror? How do you conquer? Do you conquer your health? No, you are probably going to die when it is all over. Christ becoming all in all to you is how you conquer. Let us read the rest of the list:

> *For I am persuaded, that neither death, nor life, nor angels, nor principalities, nor powers, nor things present, nor things to come, nor height, nor depth, nor any other creature, shall be able to separate us from the love of God, which is in Christ Jesus our Lord.* (vv. 38–39)

If you understand that nothing can separate you from Christ and that Christ in you is the conqueror, then you are ready to live. You are ready to live with all that the C & S gang may bring upon you.

Let us now go to Paul's next awful list in 1 Corinthians 4:9–16. In this list, he introduces us to the fact that we are living epistles known and read of all men when we manifest the Christ that is in us (2 Cor. 3:1–3). Paul told us that we birth the gospel in others because we ourselves are an epistle known and read of all men. *"For I think that God hath set forth us the apostles last, as it were appointed to death: for we are made a spectacle unto the world, and to angels and to men"* (1 Cor. 4:9). Why would Paul say we are a spectacle to angels? Angels consider us strange because we have another person, Christ, in us. The Scriptures say angels don't understand our salvation (1 Peter 1:12). We have been rebirthed by God and are not like Israel, who was only created creatures, not yet rebirthed. We are God's own children, His direct offspring, and so it is said that we are a spectacle in this world.

Continuing with 1 Corinthians 4:10–13,

We are fools for Christ's sake, but ye are wise in Christ; we are weak, but ye are strong; ye are honorable, but we are despised. Even unto this present hour we both hunger, and thirst, and are naked, and are buffeted, and have no certain dwellingplace; and labor, working with our own hands: being reviled, we bless; being persecuted, we suffer it: Being defamed, we intreat: we are made as the filth of the world, and are the offscouring of all things unto this day.

I think you would agree this is quite a list!

Verses 14–16 say,

I write not these things to shame you, but as my beloved sons I warn you. For though ye have ten thousand instructors in Christ, yet have ye not many fathers: for in Christ Jesus I have begotten you through the gospel. Wherefore I beseech you, be ye followers of me.

Do you know what has happened to us? It is an exaggerated figure, I am sure, but we have had 10,000 instructors; all of them were Christian, and all of them were in Christ. They instructed us as to what we ought to do. Have you not had many people in your life tell you what you ought to do? When people tell you what you ought to do, they have power over you; they put you under their law. Your mother probably said, *If you don't do what I'm telling you to do, I'm going to spank you.* That was law. (At a young age, this might be necessary.) Your schoolteacher said, *If you don't learn this, you are going to have to stay after school.* That was law. Preachers said, *If you don't live our doctrine, you are going to be put out of our church and maybe go to hell.* That was law. All your instructors, though they may have been born again, did not know who they were; and they taught that you had to do something in order to be someone aside from being the offspring of God that you had already become. Paul said although you had 10,000 of these instructors, you have not many fathers. Paul said he is one of these fathers because he had begotten them through the gospel. He also said, *Be followers of me and birth this gospel in others.* What does a father do? He births his own kind.

Let us go to another of Paul's lists in 2 Corinthians 4:7–12. *"But we have this treasure in earthen vessels, that the excellency of the power may be of God, and not of us"* (v. 7). Each of us is a clay pot. God wants us to know about this treasure we have in clay pots. When the C & S gang pushes us to Christ, they have to go through our flesh and that hurts. Yet, that is a part of the gospel. This is so *"that the excellency of the power may be of God, and not of us."* The old gospel made the excellency of power ours, to show the excellency of our power. For example, if you had enough faith, you received your miracle; and if you became righteous enough, God would use you. Now, in the new gospel, the excellency of power is to be of God and not of us.

Verses 8–9 say,

We are troubled on every side, yet not distressed; we are perplexed, but not in despair; persecuted, but not forsaken; cast down, but not destroyed." Have you ever been in a place like that? More than likely you kept going on "because greater is he that is in you, than he that is in the world. (1 John 4:4)

Verses 10–11 say,

Always bearing about in the body the dying of the Lord Jesus, that the life also of Jesus might be made manifest in our body. For we which live are always delivered unto death for Jesus' sake, that the life also of Jesus might be made manifest in our mortal flesh.

You might say, *I am dying! Somebody help me! I'm dying!* Jesus inside of you says, *Good! You are doing that for my sake. You are learning me; you are coming to be who you were meant to be in your human form.* Then verse 12 says, *"So then death worketh in us, but life in you."*

In 2 Corinthians 6:4–10, we have a list that tells us how we are *bona fide* children of God. *"But in all things approving ourselves as the ministers of God, in much patience, in afflictions, in necessities, in distresses"* (v. 4). A minister of God—that is what you are. We are ministers of God *"in much patience."* The

Scripture did not say in a pulpit. You are a minister of God in your patience. The verse then says *"in afflictions."* I am sure you have had tears in your eyes when you came into contact with someone else who had a burden into which you poured yourself. This is ministering in afflictions. Then you are *"in necessities."* When someone asks for prayer, and you are in a far greater need than they are, you usually go ahead and pray for them. This is how you are a minister in necessities. Added to this, verse 5 says you are a minister by Christ in you *"in stripes, in imprisonments, in tumults, in labours, in watchings, in fastings."*

Verses 6–10 give other ways we minister:

By pureness, by knowledge, by longsuffering, by kindness, by the Holy Ghost, by love unfeigned, by the word of truth, by the power of God, by the armour of righteousness on the right hand and on the left, by honour and dishonour, by evil report and good report: as deceivers, and yet true; as unknown, and yet well known; as dying, and, behold, we live; as chastened, and not killed; as sorrowful, yet always rejoicing; as poor, yet making many rich; as having nothing, and yet possessing all things.

This list is going to be real to you every day. You are going to be in worse shape than somebody else who comes your way, and you need to be ready to minister! You may be hurting more than they are. You may have a greater distress than they do. Maybe you are poorer than they are. You must remember, *Of course, I can't do it; it isn't in me to do it!* That is the whole message; it is He in you who can do it!

Sometimes you minister by the Word of Truth, sometimes by the power of God, sometimes by the armor of righteousness, sometimes by dishonor as well as honor, sometimes by evil report and good report. You minister through all these things, or rather He does! As you live through the kind of situations in this list, Christ is manifested.

Paul's final list is found in 2 Corinthians 11:22–30. *"Are they Hebrews? So am I. Are they Israelites? So am I. Are they the seed of Abraham? So am I. Are they ministers of Christ? (I speak as a fool) I am more"* (vv. 22–23). Now, here we go again as ministers. What is a minister of Christ? What Christ? The Christ who is in me; I am a minister of the Christ in me. Paul said,

> *In labours more abundant, in stripes above measure, in prisons more frequent, in deaths oft. Of the Jews five times received I forty stripes save one. Thrice was I beaten with rods, once was I stoned, thrice I suffered shipwreck, a night and a day I have been in the deep; in journeyings often, in perils of waters, in perils of robbers, in perils by mine own countrymen, in perils by the heathen, in perils in the city, in perils in the wilderness, in perils in the sea, in perils among false brethren.* (vv. 23–26)

Look at the perilous life Paul lived!

> *In weariness and painfulness, in watchings often, in hunger and thirst, in fastings often, in cold and nakedness. Beside those things that are without, that which cometh upon me daily, the care of all the churches. Who is weak, and I am not weak? Who is offended, and I burn not? If I must needs glory, I will glory of the things which concern mine infirmities.* (vv. 17–30).

Those hard times you have been experiencing could have been points of ministry! You may have forgotten that Christ is in you!

In 2 Corinthians 12:7–11, Paul wrote about a thorn in his flesh. He said that because God had given him the revelation that Christ lived in him, God had allowed him to have a thorn in the flesh. Whatever that thorn was, it was enough to daily give him a consciousness of Christ in him. Only Paul had this happen to him in the Scriptures. Abraham had no thorn in the flesh, so he went into the flesh and with Sarah birthed a child illegitimate to God's plan. Noah disobeyed God because he had no thorn in the flesh. Moses was not allowed to go into Canaan because he had no thorn in the flesh. Samson disobeyed God because he had no thorn in the flesh. David ended up killing a man and committing adultery because he had no thorn in the flesh. Need I say more?

What is this thorn in the flesh to the Apostle Paul? It was a reminder that he had received a great revelation. It is as if God said, *I will not let you forget it. I am going to remind you of it every day.* Every time Paul had this pain, this hurt, this mental stress, it was to remind him of this great revelation he had received. Do you get it? A thorn in the flesh is better than a miracle healing. It is better to have something to remind you that you are not free of the knowledge that Christ lives in you. We need to get firm in our minds that this message is what life is all about. *"And he said unto me, My grace is sufficient for thee: for my strength is made perfect in weakness"* (2 Cor. 12:9). If you like the message of grace, this is a part of it. One side of the coin of grace says all you have to do to be saved is believe on the Lord Jesus Christ. The other side of the coin is that you are going to have a thorn in the flesh; nevertheless, His grace is sufficient because His strength is made perfect in your weakness.

All my life I preached to get saints stronger in the Lord. Now I would like to get them weaker be-

cause when they are weak, then they are strong
through Christ.

> *For my strength is made perfect in weakness.
> Most gladly therefore will I rather glory in in-
> firmities, that the power of Christ may rest
> upon me. Therefore I take pleasure in infirmi-
> ties, in reproaches, in necessities, in
> persecutions, in distresses for Christ's sake: for
> when I am weak, then am I strong. I am become
> a fool in glorying; ye have compelled me: for I
> ought to have been commended of you: for in
> nothing am I behind the very chiefest apostles,
> though I be nothing.* (2 Cor. 12:9–11)

Only Paul brought us this message. It is honest
and true. His grace is sufficient while you are in these
situations. He will use them to bless others while at the
same time He will remind you daily of the great revelation He has given you.

Chapter 4
Review Questions

1. Ephesians 1:4 states, *"According as he hath
   chosen us in him before the foundation of the
   world."* When we read the Scriptures, where
   would you expect to find the details and fulfillment of this plan God had before the
   foundation of the world?

2. The *"gospel of circumcision"* can be described
   by such words as *law, Peter's gospel,* and *the
   gospel to the Jews.* Write down as many expressions as you can to describe the "gospel of
   uncircumcision."

3. To which of the two gospels mentioned in
   question #2 does each of the following statements belong?

a. If you have enough faith, God will work in the outer things and deliver you.

b. God depends on Christ in you to do an inner work and overcome everything.

4. What is the purpose of our circumstances and situations in this life?

They caught Paul and Silas, and drew them into the marketplace unto the rulers ... saying, These men, being Jews, do exceedingly trouble our city. ... the magistrates ... commanded to beat them. And when they had laid many stripes upon them, they cast them into prison.
(Acts 16:19–23)

CHAPTER 5
Paul and the Law

Introduction

It becomes obvious as we read the Scriptures that the Lord chose the Apostle Paul to bring a special message to the world. It is ironic that the Lord went to the trouble of choosing the Apostle Paul. Of course, nothing is too difficult for God, but He did go to a lot of bother in calling Paul, especially since He already had many other preachers available. Why would He choose Paul when He already had Peter, James, John, Apollos, Barnabas, and Doctor Luke, who were trained preachers or teachers? Why mess around with the Apostle Paul, the meanest man who was destroying people who followed Jesus?

The Choice of Messenger

Why didn't the Lord choose one who followed Jesus to be the spokesman for the New Testament Church and finally the message of grace? My guess is because apostles such as Peter, James, or John knew Jesus of Nazareth; they had walked and talked with Him and had been a part of His ministry. Knowing Him in the flesh would interfere with learning Christ as He lived within them. Their familiarity with Jesus and their distraction with Jesus' outer ministry to Israel would have made it difficult for them to not commingle the old message of law with the new message of grace, which they eventually did. Everything Jesus of Nazareth did was to fulfill the law. His entire message was a law message, as was His purpose, for He said in His own words, *"I am not come to destroy the law ... but to fulfil"* (Matt. 5:17). He did this by His parables and everything He taught in the kingdom message, all of which was for the restoration of Israel. Jesus was dedicated to the law. However, it is my personal conclusion that at the end of His ministry He veered away from total law and began to build a bridge to grace.

God's Choice of Paul

Paul knew nothing but the law, which helps us understand why the Lord chose the Apostle Paul. He knew nothing but Judaism. He was academically the best-trained man in the Scriptures. Paul was a rabbi, a lawyer, and someone who fulfilled everything Judaism demanded. Paul knew nothing about the ministry of Jesus of Nazareth other than what he had been told. Paul was a man who could be trained in the new message of grace, which was the antithesis to the law of Judaism. Therefore, I think the Lord chose Paul because the earthly ministry of Jesus of Nazareth, which was to the nation of Israel, did not heavily influence him.

The Law as a Divisive Force in Christianity

It probably has not occurred to you, but there is a reason why there is so much divisiveness in Christianity. I am a former Baptist, and in the encyclopedia I noted that there are 360 diverse Baptist groups in the world! There probably is very little difference among any of them, but there is enough difference that they will not fellowship with each other. Why is there so little unity in Christian circles? One explanation could be that power and money, which rule the world, also rule religion, and so divisions and problems are inevitable. It boils down to numbers and money. From the human perspective, if you have numbers, you are declared to be highly successful; and if you don't have numbers, something is wrong with what you are doing. Actually, the people who go on in the Lord are usually delivered from accumulating large numbers of followers or donations because they find out there are a whole lot of other people standing alone. Standing alone is not a big problem to on-going believers, but it is a problem in religion, generally speaking, for religion really has no place for these people.

I believe this issue of divisiveness in religion has deeper roots than the worldly struggle over power and money, and, once again, Paul shows us where this disunity originated.

Paul had several great confrontations in his life which I think were bitter and difficult. Every one of them was over the issue of law. Paul never had a problem over God's grace. It is the same today. I never hear of people who are in grace who kick others out of their fellowship. It is always the law that separates and divides us. We welcome anyone to our Christ-life meetings; we like to think that we know a little bit about grace. In law there is only divisiveness because that is the very center of law. The Apostle Paul had the supreme test of battling law. When this gospel went to the Gentiles, it was a gospel that had no law in it. It was easy dealing with the Gentiles, but at the same time the Lord told Paul to tell Israel that this is their opportunity to be saved also! That is how the Jewish person comes into the plan of God today. The earthly kingdom is set aside and will not be restored until the Millennium. The same message that went to the Gentiles, without the law, also went to Israel.

During Paul's time, two inconceivable things took place. Paul, a man who knew nothing but law, converted to God's grace. At the same time, Paul had to go to a people so deeply steeped in law and committed to it that they would kill to maintain their law. To make sure you hear it clearly, read these words in Ephesians 2:15: *"Having abolished in his flesh the enmity, even the law of commandments contained in ordinances ... so making peace."* Also read Colossians 2:14, *"Blotting out the handwriting of ordinances that was against us, which was contrary to us, and took it out of the way, nailing it to his cross."* If grace is mixed with law, then grace is no longer grace.

If you read the Scriptures as they are written, you will see something important about the law. A vessel of God can use the law to destroy other vessels of God to reach its own ends. Law-religion is devious because it has an indefinable salvation. I am not saying you cannot be saved in a law church, because you can. If you believe on the Lord Jesus Christ, you are saved. Usually a law church will not acknowledge your salvation until they say you are saved. For example, in Roman Catholicism, in order to be saved you must follow their catechism, and if you fulfill the sacraments of the church, they say you can go to heaven. That is a strong hold on people and a very indefinable salvation.

Let us look at the Baptists, of which I was a part for some time. They say you can be saved without being baptized in water, but you cannot be one of us. On the other hand, my Church of Christ friends say to be saved you not only must be baptized in water, moreover, it has to be by their preacher and in their baptistery. That narrows things down again. We also have the holiness people, who never really do get saved since they are being saved over and over again. After I was a Baptist, I decided I would try something holier, and I found myself having to be saved every time I went to a church. All of these plans of salvation are under law. Pentecostals, Charismatics, Catholics, Baptists, and many other denominations, all have agendas that require you to do something in order to be saved, and such agendas are embedded in the law.

Law is the oil for the machinery of religion. Grace is opposite to the law because grace is definable. Grace is a person. The more you know Christ, the more you understand God's plan of salvation. Grace has nothing to do with what you do and nothing to do with what you don't do. It has to do with a person. That is why Paul's message is, *"For I determined not to know any thing among you, save Jesus Christ, and him crucified"* (1 Cor. 2:2). *"But ye have not so learned Christ"* (Eph. 4:20). Paul is always turning us back to the fact that the more you know Christ the better off you are as a Christian.

In contrast to law, grace is definable because it hinges on a person. It does not hinge on what you do but on what He did. When you get that fixed in your mind, then you don't have to worry about salvation anymore. Law does not accept grace because law operates on the principle that says, *You must do what we tell you to do. You are saved and have grace because you did what we told you to do.* That approach is contrary to the very word *grace.* Law has an indefinable kind of salvation, always dependent on some human creed that is as changeable as humans are changeable. Grace is based simply on Acts 16:31, *"Believe on the Lord Jesus Christ, and thou shalt be saved."* Law cannot accept people on this basis alone; it puts them on probation in catechism, in study groups, or in learning the doctrine of that particular group. Their salvation or acceptance is contingent on these activities plus water baptism.

Trouble in the Church

Let us look at some Scriptures in Galatians 2:11–12,

But when Peter was come to Antioch, I [Paul] withstood him to the face, because he was to be blamed. For before that certain came from James, he did eat with the Gentiles: but when they were come, he withdrew and separated himself, fearing them which were of the circumcision.

I want you to circle the word *James* because we have introduced to us here a leader of the law. We see a wonderful thing take place in these verses. Peter has now seen that circumcision is no longer a needful thing to be saved. You must understand that believers out of the first Pentecostal Church of Jerusalem were circumcision believers—that is they believed they had to follow Jewish law as well as Jesus of Nazareth. The man, James, mentioned here is the pastor of that church, and is also the half-brother of Jesus. Before the believers from James' church came to Antioch, Peter was having a good time. Liberty had come and he was fellowshipping with the Gentiles. He was eating with them, although the law did not permit him to do so. Peter had made a reversal in his life, but suddenly someone said the believers from Jerusalem had arrived, and Peter made a complete change back to his old ways. When he heard the circumcision crowd from Jerusalem was there, he jumped up from the table and turned against the Gentiles in Antioch. Why did Peter do that? It seems clear to me that brother James was not going to let anyone preach grace, even if it was way off in Antioch, Greece. Therefore, James had sent a group of spies to check things out. In Galatians 2:4, Paul said, *"And that because of false brethren unawares brought in, who came in privily to spy out our liberty which we have in Christ Jesus, that they might bring us into bondage."*

Now keep in mind it was believers who were doing that! Peter was like many Christians today. They preach a lot of law mixed with a little grace. However, Peter continued under the influence of the gospel Paul preached and did eventually grow in grace until time caught up with him and he was killed. When the day came that he understood grace, he had many wonderful things to say. He saw that the incorruptible seed in us is Christ, placed there in the birthing (1 Peter 1:23). He saw that we are partakers of the God-nature that comes through the birthing (2 Peter 1:4). Peter saw some of the deep things of God and wrote about them. We give him credit for that. However, at this juncture in the Church, during the Acts period, he had reverted back to the old and there was nothing but disruption.

Law bleeds us of truth, and it takes us out of the grace of God and back to having to do something to be a child of God. When that happens, we are attempting to re-crucify Jesus. We are trying to kill Him again because we are acting as though His first death did not work.

In the eighth chapter of Acts, there is a word you need to mark in your Bible because it is something that is going on today. Acts 8:1 says,

> *And Saul was consenting unto his death.* [Saul of Tarsus consented to the death of Stephen] *and at that time there was a great persecution against the church which was at Jerusalem; and they were all scattered abroad throughout the regions of Judaea and Samaria, except the apostles.*

The word to mark is *scattered*. With the stoning of Stephen, the Church had been scattered. This was a major event that spread the message of grace. This scattering was a God-thing. Sometimes we think when there is trouble in the Church that it is bad, but it may in fact be good. Although we all hate our church troubles, the fact is that when you decide to go on in the Lord, and you are locked in with those who don't want to continue growing, there will be a scattering. People are going to be pushed off to other places. If you are not getting along with someone in your church fellowship, you need to make it right. But if it is a dispute over truth, then scattering is good. God will bless you, and He will move you to a place where you can grow.

James, an Unusual Man

Our discussion of the law comes down to one man, whom I want to tell you about because he is the most important man in the New Testament concerning the law. There is very little said about him, but what is said is very pointed. As stated earlier, James, the half-brother of Jesus of Nazareth, was behind the circumcision group in the first Church of Jerusalem. He is the person who caused most of the trouble. My purpose in discussing James is to help you see something you may not have seen before because you are going to find counterparts to it in your own walk in God.

> *And he* [Jesus] *went out from thence, and came into his own country;* [He is in His own home town of Nazareth] *and his disciples follow him. And when the Sabbath day was come, he began to teach in the synagogue:* [This is his home church where he was raised] *and many hearing him were astonished.* (Mark 6:1–2, author's words added)

When we read the word *astonished*, we think, *Isn't that great!* However, that is not what is meant by this statement. Why were they astonished? He was not preaching the strict Law of Moses. So they said, *Where did He get this stuff, where did He get this message?* Jesus was preaching the kingdom message, which was a law message, but He had made radical changes. For instance, in one place a woman was taken in adultery. Moses and his law had said that for grievous offences like adultery, she should be stoned. Jesus forgave her! That was different. *"And many hearing him were astonished, saying, From whence hath this man these things? and what wisdom is this which is given unto him, that even such mighty works are wrought by his hands"* (v. 2). When we read this portion of Scripture, we usually only see the statement of the *"mighty works."* Praise God He performed these mighty works;

but remember, He is in a hostile group, in His home church, with His rabbi in His hometown, and they are set against Him!

Looking at Mark 6:3, we see, *"Is not this the carpenter, the son of Mary, the brother of James, and Joses, and of Juda, and Simon? And are not his sisters here with us? And they were offended at him."* Here we have the first listing of four half-brothers of Jesus of Nazareth: James, Joses, Judah, and Simon. His sisters are not mentioned by name. The Scripture says Jesus' brothers and sisters were there *"and they were offended at him."* You must read this verse closely because not only the Church, but also His brothers and sisters were offended. This statement introduces something unique.

You may have wondered why the Scriptures never relate anything between the time Jesus was 12 and 30 years of age. Here we gain insight into His family. Jesus lived in a family that was offended by His ministry! How did Jesus reply to them? *"But Jesus said unto them, A prophet is not without honour, but in his own country, and among his own kin, and in his own house"* (v. 4). Jesus is talking about His own home and His own kin, which means His relatives and immediate family.

Mark 6:5–6 continue: *"And he could there do no mighty work, save that he laid his hands upon a few sick folk, and healed them. And he marveled because of their unbelief, and he went round about the villages, teaching."* What a strange story this is. It tells us Jesus had no honor from His family. Nowhere in the Scriptures does His family honor Him. After Canaan of Galilee, there is never a word spoken by Mary to the credit of Jesus. What is behind all this? Can you believe God sent His Son to earth through a 14-year-old girl, who birthed Him and bore several other children, and she would become so locked into law that she and her family would literally reject what Jesus was sent to do?

Luke 2:42–45 say,

And when he was twelve years old, they went up to Jerusalem after the custom of the feast. And when they had fulfilled the days, as they returned, the child Jesus tarried behind in Jerusalem; and Joseph and His mother knew not of it.

It would be helpful to underline the words *Joseph and His mother knew not of it.* *"But they, supposing him to have been in the company, went a day's journey; and they sought him among their kinsfolk and acquaintance. And when they found him not, they turned back again to Jerusalem, seeking him."* This is the place in the Scriptures where I found the title for one of my previous books, *Jesus Lost in the Church.*

And it came to pass, that after three days they found him in the temple, sitting in the midst of the doctors, both hearing them, and asking them questions. And all that heard him were astonished at his understanding and answers. And when they saw him, they were amazed: and his mother said unto him, Son, why hast thou thus dealt with us? behold, thy father and I have sought thee sorrowing. (Luke 2:46–48)

When Doctor Luke penned verse 43 he said, *"Joseph and his mother knew not of it,"* but when Mary spoke in verse 48 she said, *"Thy father and I have sought thee sorrowing."* Mary stated that Joseph was His father! In a way, that was not a bad thing to do. If I adopted a child, I would want that child to call me father, and I would be that child's father. That sets well, with one exception. Look at the next verse, which is verse 49, *"And he said unto them, How is it that ye sought me? Wist ye not that I must be about my Fa-*

ther's business?" This is a real clarification, and it comes through as a rebuke to Mary who had said, *Your father and I have been looking for you.* Jesus said, *I have been about my Father's business.* Do you think perhaps family life had become so mixed up with religion and law that Mary was doing her best to make Jesus one of her sons like all the rest of them? She had four other sons. Perhaps Jesus was no different than the others to her.

Mary appears to have forgotten that the angel had told her the details of how she would birth the Savior of her people (Luke 1:26–38). Had she forgotten that she knew no man when this took place? Had she forgotten the virgin birth and being visited by angels? Had she forgotten the birthing in Bethlehem and then two years later the three wise men who came? Had she forgotten Zechariah and Elizabeth, who pointedly had a part of the birthing of Jesus by the coming of John the Baptist as forerunner? Had she forgotten Simeon and Anna who had prophesied over the child? Had she forgotten all these events? I am not saying she did, but what I am suggesting is that if she had forgotten, the problem was the law and legalism of her Judiaistic religion. Mary could not go against what was taught in the temple by the rabbi or what was taught in Moses' law. She was bound to it. The facts, as I see them, are that Jesus had no support from His family!

In Mark chapter 3:14–19, we have another interesting sidelight.

And he [Jesus] ordained twelve, that they should be with him, and that he might send them forth to preach, and to have power to heal sicknesses, and to cast out devils: And Simon he surnamed Peter; and James the son of Zebedee, and John the brother of James; and he surnamed them Boanerges, which is, the sons of thunder. And

*Andrew, and Philip, and Bartholomew, and
Matthew, and Thomas, and James the son of
Alphaeus, and Thaddaeus, and Simon the Ca-
naanite, and Judas Iscariot, which also
betrayed him: and they went into an house.*

You will notice that two men named James are mentioned, James the son of Zebedee and John's brother
and James the son of Alpheus. This is the calling and
the naming of the twelve apostles. Continuing with
verse 20, *"And the multitude cometh together again, so
that they could not so much as eat bread. And when his
friends heard of it...."* You can turn to any of the leading translators and you will find that usually when they
deal with the word *friends* it means family. If you have
a Bible that gives you footnote information on this
Greek word for *friends*, it will usually say "family,
kinsmen, kinfolk or relative." So, let us read it as suggested. It says His relatives heard He had appointed
twelve men to be apostles, and *"they went out to lay
hold on him: for they said, He is beside himself"* (v. 21).
If you read this material in the original language it
would say something like this: *And when His relatives
heard that He had named twelve apostles, they alone
having the power to commit Him* (under Jewish law, the
family had the power to commit an insane person)*, they
went up to lay hold of Him for they thought He was crazy!* His family thought Jesus was crazy because He
appointed twelve apostles! But did you notice who was
missing in the naming of the twelve men? There was no
mention of James, His brother, Joses, Judah, or Simon.
He listed none of His own family. Many Bible scholars
have said that is what made His family bitter. The law
says the only way He could be incarcerated or put in a
place for the insane would be by His own family. It appears here that His family had started out to do just that.

Go with me to John 7, where we will read some
very interesting text. I hope you have a King James

Bible because others don't translate this text in a forthright manner. *"After these things Jesus walked in Gali-Galilee: for he would not walk in Jewry, because the Jews sought to kill him"* (John 7:1). Jewry is Jerusalem or Judea. Jesus knew He could not go there because the Jews were set to kill Him. You would be amazed to know that in the Gospel of John alone, 20 times the statement is made that someone tried to kill Jesus. Verses 2–3 continue: *"Now the Jews' feast of tabernacles was at hand. His brethren...."* We need to stop here and establish who His brethren are. Again, His brethren are His immediate family. The Greek word for *brethren* used by the gospel writers (Matthew, Mark, Luke, and John) means "family." I make a point of this because, in the epistles, when you are called a brother, it means you have been rebirthed and are in the family of God. These people, however, were not rebirthed; they were not born again.

The brethren mentioned here in the Greek always meant His own family, so the text actually says, *"His* [family] *therefore said unto Him, Depart hence, and go into Judea"* (John 7:3). Let us stop right here! Would you like to have a family that would send you where they know the Jews are going to kill you? What kind of a family is it that would tell Jesus to go over to Judea and show them some of His miracles? That is a trap! *"Depart hence, and go into Judea, that thy disciples also may see the works that thou doest. For there is no man that doeth anything in secret, and he himself seeketh to be known openly. If thou do these things, show thyself to the world. For neither did His* [family] *believe in Him"* (vv. 3–5). Are you developing a concern about His family?

"Then Jesus said unto them [His family]*, My time is not yet come: but your time is alway ready"* (John 7:6). Jesus could not agree to go into Judea because He knew there was only one specific day of the year that

He could die. That day had to be the Passover. He could not take a chance of going into Judea, or anywhere else, where His family might thwart the plan of God.

When you read the Scriptures, did you ever wonder why Jesus ran away from the crowd, or why He went into the mountains, the desert, or a boat? Now we can see that He was most likely trying to get away from His family and His enemies! In the past, I have preached that Jesus had to get alone to pray. Now I see that He was also trying to save His life! He could only die at the Passover.

There is something else He said that is important. *"But your time is alway ready. The world cannot hate you; but me it hateth, because I testify of it, that the works thereof are evil"* (John 7:6–7). This is a very strong prophetic word. He is speaking this to His own family! Did you know that when His half-brother James became the head of the Church at Jerusalem, he was loved by the world? Peter, who was the head of the early church body, was killed. Paul was killed and the Apostle James was killed. All the apostles except one were eventually killed for the message. But there was one fellow who survived it all, James, the half-brother of Jesus. And Jesus prophesied here, *"the world cannot hate you"* (v. 7). It is implied in that statement that Jesus' half-brother James had gone with the world, and he would be the means by which the Apostle James would be killed. History records it was collaboration between James and Herod that caused the death of the Apostle James.

An additional portion of Scripture we should look at is John 19:25–27,

> *Now there stood by the cross of Jesus his mother, and his mother's sister, Mary the wife of Cleophas, and Mary Magdalene. When Jesus therefore saw his mother, and the disciple*

standing by, whom he loved [John], *he saith unto his mother, Woman, behold thy son! Then
saith he to the disciple, Behold thy mother! And
from that hour that disciple took her unto his
own home.*

Now this is a very interesting sidelight. I wonder
where His four brothers were when He was hanging on
the cross. They are not mentioned at all, but Mary was
there. History records that Joseph was dead. Jesus was
responsible for His mother according to Jewish law.
Instead of Jesus handing Mary over to the next oldest
son, He turned to a non-family person, John. He said
He wanted John to take over the care of His mother. It
was James' responsibility, but very pointedly Jesus
turned her over to John.

Once I was on a sightseeing trip in the Aegean
Sea. On one particular day, we went to Ephesus. As
part of the tour we were going to see where Paul
preached. There were some ruins in the area, and one
of them was reported to be Mary's home. How in the
world did Mary get over to Ephesus, such a long way
from Jerusalem? There was a plaque stating that some
of the ruins were the home that John the apostle had
built for Mary. John took Mary away from Jerusalem
and away from her family. John had provided a home
for Mary where she lived out her days. How many
daughters did Mary have? How many sons-in-law did
she have? How many wives did these four sons have?
Yet, John took her and cared for her until she died.
What a strange paradox to have a non-family member
take care of Mary when there were so many family
members available.

If you read closely in the book of Acts, from about
the seventh chapter on, you will see again and again the
name of James coming up. Remember, James was in
charge of the circumcision party out of the first Pente-

costal Church in Jerusalem, and he is the one who sent men out to watch what Paul was doing (Gal. 2:4, 12). When Paul reported to the apostles and elders in Jerusalem, you will notice in Acts 15:13 and 19 that James appears to be in charge. Tradition supports the New Testament picture of James as a man of great influence and intense piety according to Jewish ideals. Also, it is believed that he never ceased to keep the Jewish law with rigor and care. In my wildest speculation, I tried to figure out how a man like that got to be in charge of the first Pentecostal Church. I studied every book I could find, and I was still left with this same question: How did James get to be over Peter and the other apostles? History further records that he came to political power and joined with Herod to cause the death of James the apostle. We can read of the turmoil that continued in religion in those days. I ask also, why would anyone want to kill Paul? I think it was because men want to prove themselves to be something within themselves. Consequently, when Paul came with the gospel that says, *I am crucified—I no longer live,* that was an affront to their very identity and men rejected it and became violent. Violence, rather than love, has reigned throughout the history of the Christian Church because of law. The second reason I mention this is because I want you to cheer up and realize that your family is not so bad after all! For 30 years Jesus lived in the tyranny of a family, a church, a pastor, and a town that did not agree with Him. I would like to see that Christ become the life of born-again believers in my day before religion is able to destroy the opportunity. History proves that Satan will do anything to keep believers from knowing Christ is the new-creation life.

A preacher said to me one time, "Litzman, if I preached grace, there would not be anyone who would come back to church. They would just live on their own." I thought, how deceived you are to God's grace and to the message of the New Testament. When people fall in love with the Christ in them, they serve God differently than they ever did before. You could not keep them from fellowship. You may keep them from church programs, as they don't want those any more. You may keep them from building buildings, as they are tired of that. Nevertheless, you are not going to keep them from fellowship or from loving one another.

A last thought about James. How is it that those who chose the Scriptures as we now have them would have chosen an epistle written by this man? He did say some good things in his epistle. He gave us the best teaching on temptation to be found in the Scriptures, as far as I have found. Also, one of the most enlightened verses I use comes out of James where he said, *"Therefore to him that knoweth to do good, and doeth it not, to him it is sin"* (James 4:17). That fits the message of grace better than any Scripture I know concerning sin. However, Paul's message does not fit the Judaistic writers. Much of Paul's message does not fit Peter, James, John, or Jude's writings. It is an antithesis to them. James said more than once that we are saved by works. I am amazed at the tiptoeing and dancing around these verses of Scripture by writers of commentaries. No one wants to take it as James wrote it. He plainly said, *"Faith without works is dead"* (James 2:14–26). Paul said you are saved by grace and not by works. These are opposing views. James and Paul were enemies. Jesus said the day would come when good people were going to kill you, thinking they did God a service. James fits into that category.

Rightly Dividing the Scriptures

I don't want you to think there is anything in your Bible that is not inspired or given by God. If you rightly divide the Scriptures, you must rightly divide between Paul's epistles and the Judaistic epistles. What do I mean by a Judaistic epistle? They are the epistles that in some way contend for the kingdom message, which is the message Paul set aside in Acts 28:28 when the gospel went to the Gentiles. The Bible is going to be studied in the tribulation period. There will not be new Scriptures because the Bible we have is the eternal Word. Our Bible is going to be studied in the new heaven and the new earth. God allowed the Judaistic epistles to be placed in it even though they are adverse to Paul's message. The Scriptures are very specific. Reading the first verse of James chapter 1: *"James, a servant of God and of the Lord Jesus Christ, to the twelve tribes which are scattered abroad, greeting."* This is not written to the born-again at all! It is not to those who believe the gospel that was revealed to Paul. It is not to grace believers at all!

God put it in the Bible because one day He is going to use it. It belongs to the twelve tribes. You and I are not in any tribe. Once born again, we are a new race of people in Christ. There are no born-again Indians, Jews, Greeks, or Gentiles. There will come a day when the Jews are going to study this material. They are going to hear what James had to say. However, you and I don't presently have a word in there for us. We can take illustrations from it and get moral help from it, but there is no spiritual food for the born-again believer in the kingdom message or in the Judaistic teachings. When I understood that, I was helped greatly. Everything in the Bible is put there for a divine purpose. There were many books and epistles that were not included in our Bible because they did not fit God's plan.

I close this chapter with this thought: If you are growing in the knowledge of the Lord, you must learn how to rightly divide the truth as Paul taught in 2 Timothy 2:15. This is necessary because not all the Scriptures speak to you. As I said, you can be blessed by the Bible and its examples morally; nevertheless, there is no life in much of it unless you see Christ because it was not a message that was spoken to you. Out of Paul's 14 epistles, 13 of them state the message is to the Gentiles. He states he is the apostle to the Gentiles (Rom. 11:13; Gal. 2:8; 1 Tim. 2:7; 2 Tim. 1:11). That is a specific message, and that is what belongs to you and me. We love all the Scriptures, but we have to be careful to rightly divide what belongs to us and what does not belong to us. If certain Scriptures dealing with the events that take place after the Rapture of the Church belong to the Jews, then leave it for the Jews to work out in the Tribulation period.

The twelve tribes will be gathered together again under the law and will not be born again until they accept their Messiah. Of course, that has nothing to do with you and I, who are a different family. We are a heavenly group. We belong in the heavens, seated with Christ (Eph. 2:6). We are rebirthed and are His offspring. Israel has never been His offspring and will not be until they accept their Messiah as a nation. Jews today who are saved are just like Gentiles. They lose their Judaism just as we lose being Gentiles (Gal. 3:28; Col. 3:11). We are children of God and birthed by Him, a new creation (2 Cor. 5:17; Gal. 6:15), a different group of people. Once that is settled in your mind, it will make your Bible the most interesting book you have ever read!

Chapter 5
Review Questions

1. In Ephesians 4:20, Paul said, *"But ye have not so learned Christ."* How do you think a Christian "learns Christ"?

2. Can law and grace co-exist at the same time in a person? Explain your answer.

3. In Galatians 2:4, Paul wrote, *"False brethren ... spy out our liberty which we have in Christ Jesus, that they might bring us into bondage."* Since the Holy Spirit has been teaching you about the Christ in you who is your only life, have you had situations come up where others have tried to return you to past bondage? Make a list of the bondage involved.

4. In what ways do you see the law working in destructive ways in the Church today?

*[The jailor] made their feet fast in the stocks ... And
suddenly there was a great earthquake, so that the foun-
dations of the prison were shaken: and immediately all
the doors were opened, and every one's bands were
loosed. And the keeper of the prison awaking out of his
sleep, and seeing the prison doors open, he drew out his
sword, and would have killed himself, supposing that the
prisoners had been fled. But Paul cried with a loud
voice, saying, Do thyself no harm: for we are all here.
Then he called for a light, and sprang in, and came
trembling, and fell down before Paul and Silas, and
brought them out, and said, Sirs, what must I do to be
saved? And they said, Believe on the Lord Jesus Christ,
and thou shalt be saved, and thy house.* (Acts 16:23–31)

CHAPTER 6
Paul and the Mind

Introduction

Ever since I had a revelation of Christ in me, it has been my conclusion that Paul's gospel has never been fully preached most of the time. The words of Paul, however, are very clear. Paul said the life we live is Christ (Gal. 2:20). In the same Scripture, he also said we no longer live; Christ lives in us. To Paul, life is a person and that person is Christ. Paul did not say he had a special emotional experience or that he received a special thrill in his salvation. He did say the Spirit revealed to him that Christ lived in him (Gal. 1:15–16). You can twist and turn that statement any way you want, but in your hunger to know God, you will have to accept the words *Christ lives in you* as being the key to the entire issue. You will not know the gospel truth unless you see Christ in this very tangible way.

Why Was Paul Chosen?

Why did God choose the Apostle Paul for this revelation? Although I raised this question in the previous chapter on "Paul and the Law," it is important to revisit it here. Great preachers personally trained by Jesus Christ were living in Paul's day. When God was ready to make this truth known, He did not use any of the existing candidates. That fact used to bother me until I was willing to scrape away the veneer of religion and look at things as I believe God does. God probably saw that anyone whom Jesus had taught was going to be preoccupied by the teaching of Jesus of Nazareth because He was the Son of God. He was

God in the flesh; how could they ever get that completely out of their minds? They would always see Je-Jesus that way. God was going to send a new message never heard before—a message so different that He did not want it commingled or mixed up with anything taught ever before. The same Jesus who had taught the apostles selected a person who knew nothing about the teaching of Jesus of Nazareth to bring this message of *"Christ in you, the hope of glory"* (Col. 1:27). I think God chose Paul because his mind was not filled with the old teaching of Jesus while on earth. In 2 Corinthians 5:16, Paul said we are to no longer know the Jesus who lived in the flesh. I am convinced that everywhere Paul went someone would say, *Yes, I knew Jesus. I saw Him after He was raised from the dead! I am one of the 500. I was there when He healed. I was there when He broke the loaves and fishes.* All these events could easily have been remembered in Paul's day. As far as I know, Paul never met Jesus of Nazareth. He knew He was a rabbi, but he did not personally know anything about Him.

Paul's Message Not of Jesus of Nazareth

Paul had another message that really had little to do with Jesus of Nazareth, except for His death, burial, resurrection, and ascension. Paul centered his attention on these four aspects of the life of Jesus of Nazareth and nothing else—not even His virgin birth. Though Paul obviously must have believed in that birth, he never mentions it. Remember that Paul did not meet God in a church meeting. He did not come to God in a general appeal. He did not come to God during an altar call with others. He did not even come to God through a personal witness from someone else. He was not won to God by the conviction of the Holy Spirit, as you and I were. Paul came to God because the Lord knocked him down, struck him blind, and hollered at him out of heaven!

God's Plan for Paul

The big thing God wanted to do through Paul was something that could not be accomplished in the ministry of Jesus of Nazareth. In fact, it was not accomplished in 1,700 years of Judaism and not even mentioned in 4,300 years of the Bible. As I understand God's plan, He created human beings incomplete. What was lacking was that our spirit was not complete without Christ in us. Paul was the one who received this message when God revealed it to him in the Arabian Desert. *"But when it pleased God, who separated me from my mother's womb, and called me by his grace, to reveal His Son in me."* (Gal. 1:15–16). These Scriptures encompass the entirety of the gospel of grace and are the foundation stone of the Christ-life message. The words focus on man coming to the knowledge, given by God, that salvation now is the fulfillment and the completion of the human being.

In Christianity, we have always made the statement that people are not what they ought to be until they become Christians. That doesn't make sense because I know there are many non-Christians who live better lives than Christians do, if you look at the outer things. What does make sense is that no human being is complete in spirit until he or she ~~accepts~~ Jesus as *Believes* Savior. Not even then do most Christians know about their completion until their minds are changed as to what life is, what it is all about, and who their life is! My life is not my own! *"I am crucified with Christ; nevertheless I live; yet not I, but Christ liveth in me"* (Gal. 2:20). My true life is another person. That is what Paul's great revelation was about. Humans are incomplete beings, created entities without Christ in them. Paul, the apostle to the Gentiles, is the one to whom God gave this great mystery: *"To whom God would make known what is the riches of the glory of this mystery among the Gentiles; which is Christ in you, the hope of glory"* (Col. 1:27). Paul opened to us what completes our life—the revelation of Christ as the only life of the believer. All human beings not born again are incomplete.

Since the Apostle Paul, this message has grown slowly and has been attacked over and again. The message was completely lost within 200 years after the death of the Apostle Paul. Romanism established a gospel based on law. Only in these last days has this message begun to be proclaimed worldwide. People all over the world are coming to the understanding of the truth that human beings are only complete by Christ in them, and this understanding is a God-thing and has nothing to do with God raising up a man or starting a movement or a denomination. The more evil the world becomes, the more important it will be that human beings understand that they are complete when they are in Christ; they can function by that knowledge. A completed human being can live in a hellish environment. By Christ in me, I have overcome death, hell, and the grave. Whatever happens, we are going to make it, but we do need to learn about this Christ who lives in us. Multitudes of Christians go after everything in an attempt to complete themselves because they don't know Christ in them is their completion. They buy every book on how to do this or that, how to be this or that, but they never come to a knowing of who they are because they are ignorant of what God's plan is and what the gospel says about them.

The Importance of the Mind

Paul came to grips with this message of *"Christ in you, the hope of glory,"* and he knew what he was doing. He introduced us to the fact that the great plan of God is finally resolved in the mind. "Spiritual growth" is actually being *"renewed in knowledge"* (Col. 3:10): *"Be ye transformed by the renewing of your mind"* (Rom. 12:2); *"And have put on the new man, which is renewed in knowledge after the image of him that created him"* (Col. 3:10); and *"Grow in grace, and in the knowledge of our Lord and Saviour Jesus Christ"* (2 Peter 3:18). It takes place in the mind because you cannot be any more spiritual in your spirit. Your spirit is perfect because Christ is in your spirit. The only place of growth for the human being is in the soul/mind. That is where *"faith is the substance of things hoped for, the evidence of things not seen"* (Heb. 11:1). *"So then faith cometh by hearing, and hearing by the word of God"* (Rom. 10:17). Faith and spirituality all center in your thinking. We are all learning more as we go along and cannot depend on what others say about the Scriptures. Since men teach different ideas about what the Scriptures say, we must have them fixed in our minds by the Holy Spirit in order to grow spiritually.

The Renewal of the Mind

Paul is the first to get us involved in renewing the mind. Four key words appear in Paul's writings: *knowledge, wisdom, understanding,* and *revelation.* All four of these involve the mind. Paul saw something no one else had ever seen. He saw that God could do the ultimate work of grace by putting Christ in the human being, yet the human being may never know it. Christians could live their entire lives with Christ in them and never know it. Paul's teaching centered on coming to that knowing. That is why Paul gives us lessons on body, soul, and spirit (1 Thess. 5:23). We are a body, we have a soul (which is our mind, our will, and our emotions) and, as rebirthed sons of God, our spirit is now in union with Christ. We are Christians or Christ-persons.

Three Aspects of Salvation

One of the most important things Paul does in all his epistles is to teach us that there are three different stages or aspects of salvation (See figure 3). Those three aspects concern spirit, soul, and body.

Three Actions of Deliverance in Salvation
2 Cor. 1:10

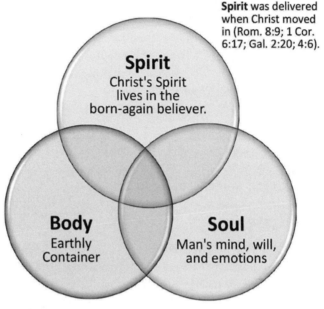

Spirit
Christ's Spirit lives in the born-again believer.

Spirit was delivered when Christ moved in (Rom. 8:9; 1 Cor. 6:17; Gal. 2:20; 4:6).

Body
Earthly Container

Soul
Man's mind, will, and emotions

Body will be delivered at the Resurrection (Rom. 8:23; 1 Cor. 15:44, 49).

Soul is continually being delivered as the mind is renewed by the Holy Spirit's teaching (Rom. 12:2; Eph. 4:13, 23; 2 Cor. 3:3; 4:16; Col. 3:10).

Figure 3

When a person is born again, you can separate spirit from the rest of the human being because it stands perfect. When God looks at a person with Christ in him, that person is perfect in His sight. *"But of him are ye in Christ Jesus, who of God is made unto us wisdom, and righteousness, and sanctification, and redemption"* (1 Cor. 1:30). That is what God sees. When you look at me, you watch what I do. When God looks at me, He sees Jesus, and He sees what Christ has done to allow Him to see Jesus in me. He sees Christ in me through the Cross. Through the Cross, I have become everything—not on my own, but through what Jesus accomplished at Calvary. The salvation of the spirit is complete. It is finished, and you cannot add to it. You cannot get more of God in you. You cannot get more of Christ in you. Christ comes into you by a birthing. When the seed, Christ, is put into a person at the birthing, no more is needed. One little seed does it all, creating a new person. Christ in you comes by *"the incorruptible seed"* (1 Peter 1:23). When it is joined to you and me, it constitutes a finished work.

The Separation of Soul and Spirit

In addition to showing us the salvation of the spirit is complete because Christ lives in us, Paul also separated soul and spirit. *"For the word of God is quick, and powerful, and sharper than any twoedged sword, piercing even to the dividing asunder of soul and spirit"* (Heb. 4:12). The Word of God separates and divides soul and spirit. Christians' failure to separate soul and spirit explains why so many never enjoy Christianity. In spirit I stand perfect before God. In soul—my mind, will, and emotions—I am not perfect. I will always be learning in the soul. There is so much more to know about this love affair we have with Jesus who is in us. When Paul separated soul and spirit, he was able to concentrate on the mind because it is one thing to have Christ in you, but it is another to know it!

In your soul, you are always in the process of being saved. We must watch our terminology here because this is a very important understanding. Our terminology to this day in Christianity is to get "souls saved" by conducting "soul-winning" crusades. That is really not proper language. It is a holdover from the Old Testament because soul and spirit were synonymous in the Old Testament. Separation between soul and spirit came when Christ was joined to us as a result of Calvary and grace. This separation does not exist in the Old Testament, so the Old Testament could say *"he that winneth souls is wise"* (Prov. 11:30). I have eternal life dwelling in me now, which is in my spirit, but in my soul I am always being saved. Also, we must remember that in body we will not be saved until the resurrection morning. Our bodies will be saved in the future. This explains the three phases of salvation found in 2 Corinthians 1:9–10.

Paul introduces us to what happens when we are born again. The goal of true Christianity is to release the Christ in you so the body and soul, which we call the human self, can be overwhelmed and expressed by spirit. Only Christians who have had a revelation that Christ is their life have an opportunity to become who God created them to be. It is not enough just to be saved. If you are not saved, you will go to hell. If you are saved, you are going to heaven regardless of what you know. However, to know who you are in this human form is a great understanding and completely changes your life on earth. God created you to be something special for Him. Christians who don't know the Christ who is in them will never come to that understanding.

The Importance of Knowing Who You Are

Many of us go from group to group, from one church to another, and from doctrine to doctrine because we don't know who we are. We are searching for our true identity. Some people think the Christ-life is ridiculous because it is so simple. Regardless of what you may think, my true self is growing up in Christ. It is Christ as me. Christ comes to live in me, and He will shine through me as I was uniquely created to reflect Him. That is actually what God wanted from the beginning, and that is what Paul understood. We have the liberty to be who we are created to be. All your life you had these little pulls on you to be yourself, and there is nothing wrong with being who you are when you know Christ is your life because that is what God created you to be. Without this revelation knowledge most humans will never become who they were created to be. You need a gospel that will change your mind about who you are, and the gospel of grace will do this for you. Nevertheless, one of the most difficult things you will ever do is to change your mind, and I want to focus on this issue in the following sections.

The Mind of Christ

Paul told us about putting on the mind of Christ: *"But we have the mind of Christ"* (1 Cor. 2:16). *"Let this mind be in you, which was also in Christ Jesus"* (Phil. 2:5). Paul said if your mind does not become compatible with the Christ in you, then Christ will never be manifested through you. Because of what they believe, the majority of God's children don't express Christ as our Father desires. Our doctrines most often keep us from manifesting Christ. If we don't have a change of mind from law-religion, then Christ in us will never have our mind to express Himself. Jesus expresses Himself through our soul—our mind, will, and emotions. When I came to the truth of this message, I tried to never again stereotype people. I never push people to sing, clap their hands, jump up and down, or do this or do that. It is not that those things are bad, but I believe Christ should come out of you as you are. Yet, if God created you so that it is natural for you to do these things, in Christ you have the liberty to do them.

We all seem to have a filter in our minds that says everything you know about Christ must come through that filter before you can accept it. Most people will not accept something in the Scriptures because they can only receive through their filter. Our doctrines are filters that cut out certain things and accept other things. We encourage believers to make it possible for Christ to flow through their minds. Once He overwhelms the mind, then the mind operates the body, and

Christian living is spontaneous. We want to grow into this spontaneous living. We want to come to the place where we don't have to get up every morning and say, *O God I want to be a good Christian today.* We just get up and say, *Jesus, here we go.*

The Gospel of Correction

Most of what we hear in Christianity today is a gospel of correction. You don't hear a gospel that says every one of you has Jesus in you and you could not be any better off spiritually than you are right now. As a born-again believer, you now stand perfect before God. Most often the preacher is not going to tell you this truth. Rather, he is going to tell you, *I know you folk are saved, but if you don't get to the Wednesday night meeting, you are not living for God as you ought to. If you don't put money in the offering, you are failing God.* The fact is the preacher doesn't have to tell me what to do because Christ lives in me. We live by love commandments. Furthermore, we should never preach anything that tells believers they are not what they ought to be if they don't do this or that. They are what they ought to be by God's finished work on the cross—not by what they do or don't do.

The Apostle Paul's message is that Christ in us will be taught to the soul and then we are going to express him in our daily living. The way God created you is the way Jesus is going to come out of you. That is the blessed liberty you and I have. Some of you are going to be quiet, and some of you are going to be loud.

Paul had the most colossal mind change of anyone I could ever imagine. I have had people tell me, *Oh, I just could not believe or understand that; I am just too old.* Or they offer some other excuse why they are stuck in their old ways. I always like to tell about a fellow who must have been about 85 years of age. He and his wife were sitting in a meeting, and he could barely hear what I was saying. Finally, when I came to the end of my teaching he looked over to his wife and said to her, "Do you think I could change at this age?" I responded to the man, "Sure you can! But," I added, "It will be the hardest thing you will ever do." A change of mind means to change your ideas about who made you, who you are, and who gave you your identity. To lose our old identity is very hard on us.

The Change of Mind in the Apostle Paul

Paul's emphasis was on how the body, soul, and spirit work. I want you to notice the mind change that came to Paul in Philippians 3:3–4:

> *For we are the circumcision, which worship God in the spirit, and rejoice in Christ Jesus,* [there is the in-Christ message right in the heart of this] *and have no confidence in the flesh. Though I might also have confidence in the flesh. If any other man thinketh that he hath whereof he might trust in the flesh, I more.*

In other words, Paul said he can boast more than anyone else about his past identity. Here is the record in verses 5–7:

> *Circumcised the eighth day, of the stock of Israel, of the tribe of Benjamin, an Hebrew of the Hebrews; as touching the law, a Pharisee; concerning zeal, persecuting the church; touching the righteousness which is in the law, blameless. But what things were gain to me, those I counted loss for Christ.*

In this passage from Philippians, we see the confession of a mind change. I hope you have a mind change yourself to see how profound a change it was and how deep were the changes Paul made to follow Christ in this way. His very physical birthing had to be set aside. He suffered the loss of parental activity in his life. He suffered the loss of his education. He suffered the loss of his ethnicity. He suffered the loss of being of the tribe of Benjamin, a Hebrew of the Hebrews. He suffered the loss of being a rabbi and a lawyer. He was a famous man among Judaism of that day because he destroyed the followers of Christ. When it came to the law, he said he was blameless. He is the only man I know in the Scriptures who ever said these things. The Scriptures say no man could keep the law, but Paul did it better than anyone else if he could say that he was blameless on this point. Paul said all these things that were gain to him, that had to do with who he was, he counted loss for Christ. Paul was not saying that he prayed for the Holy Spirit to wipe them out of his life so he would not have them anymore. He did not just get rid of all these things as if they were nothing; he suffered the loss of them for Christ. The issue was Christ. All these positions from his past gave him his identity. Paul took everything that made him who he was in the flesh and suffered the loss of it for Christ. How much of your past identity is still there, blocking Christ from living through you? He will not use your first birthing, regardless of who your earthly parents were. He is not interested in your achievements as a Rhodes Scholar, a Harvard graduate, or that you graduated summa cum laude. He is not interested in the fact that you are a famous politician, a lawyer, a homemaker, an artist, a writer, or a criminal. What loss did you suffer for Christ to be your identity? Now there is an important fact.

When I talk like this, most people say, *Well, I don't know how to get rid of all those things.* The fact is that you cannot. Everything in your mind is going to be there until your dying moment. It is like the hard disk on a computer. Everything that has ever happened to you is still there. You don't remember most of it; but once in a while something is triggered, and you have a memory of it. Your objective, therefore, is not to ask God to get rid of your past but to suffer the loss of these things for Christ. In other words, you allow Christ to be more important than your past. That is hard on believers because they say, *Well, I was trained a certain way.* Suffer the loss of it in your thinking, and I promise you that later on Jesus as you may use it. You might say, *Well I was born right; I was born* (Italian, German, French, Mexican, African-American, or any other ethnicity*), and we are the greatest.* Suffer the loss of it, and Jesus will come through your ethnic ways. He wants you to suffer the loss of your identity so Christ can use you as you were created. That takes a mind change.

Let us read on in verse 8:

Yea doubtless, and I count all things but loss for the excellency of the knowledge of Christ Jesus my Lord: for whom I have suffered the loss of all things, and do count them but dung, that I may win Christ.

This is one of the most loaded verses in the whole Bible. Paul said, *"I count all things but loss."* They are not gone, but counted as loss. They are no longer on his profit side. Many believers say, *Well, I cannot be who I am without incorporating all of this into who I am.* Paul said the very opposite, *"I have suffered the loss of these things."* But notice the verse takes us deeper and tells us how he suffered this loss. Paul stated, *"I count all things but loss for the excellency of the knowledge."* This knowledge takes us right back to the mind. Paul had said, *I am not going to talk about my parents anymore. They were rich. They educated me well. I suffer the loss of all that "for the excellency of the knowledge of Christ Jesus my Lord."*

One day I prayed a prayer like that about my past. Most of it was not so great anyhow, but I depended on it. Since I had been in a number of colleges and universities, I had some education. I had to suffer the loss of that. I hope He can use what I know, but I suffer the loss of that as my identity, the thing that makes me who I am. I would rather tell you of the knowledge of Christ Jesus my Lord than to tell you about my education. The reason I now think this way is because that was not the real me. I had long thought that was the real me, but none of that completed my creation. Only being in Christ completed me (Col. 2:10). The real me now is Christ in me. I still have all that has ever happened to me in my mind-computer. I know it is still there. I remember it sometimes, and Christ comes through it. But that is not what makes me who I am. I am who I am by the Christ who is in me.

When someone says to me, *Well, you are telling these people they don't have to do anything to be saved,* I leave it right there because I know they don't understand the separation of body, soul, and spirit. I tell them, *You are absolutely right; you cannot do one blessed thing to be saved. You cannot add anything to it. All you can do is believe on the Lord Jesus Christ to be saved.* There is nothing you can do, but when you get down to the nitty-gritty I say, *Salvation is in my spirit.* In spirit is where your eternal life is; and since salvation is a person (Rom. 5:10), it is perfect because Christ stands perfect before God as me (1 Cor. 1:30). This means you are ready to meet the Lord at any time; but in your mind (soul), you will still be growing. The soul is where you learn things, decide things, and do things, and that is where the Holy Spirit works to teach and guide us. He works strictly in the soul. Religious teaching can be confusing on this point because too often religion erroneously teaches that the Holy Spirit takes Christ's place in believers. No Scripture supports that notion. All spiritual growth takes place in the soul/mind. Paul clearly stated, *"For the excellency of the knowledge of Christ Jesus my Lord"* (Phil. 3:8). Paul did not say for the excellency of the life of Christ. He did not say for the excellency of the Spirit of Christ. He did not say for the excellency of the eternal life of Christ. He said for the excellency of knowledge! Spiritual maturity is a knowing, and it takes place in the mind.

I believe you can change your mind about anything if you want to do so. However, your mind is committed to doing things in a certain way, and it will hurt if you don't follow that original pattern, even though it is wrong. The Apostle Paul came back again and again with a single remedy for this:

- *"Let this mind be in you, which was also in Christ Jesus"* (Phil. 2:5).

- *"But we have the mind of Christ"* (1 Cor. 2:16).

- *"Be ye transformed by the renewing of your mind"* (Rom. 12:2).

- *"And be renewed in the spirit of your mind"* (Eph. 4:23).

- *"And have put on the new man, which is renewed in knowledge after the image of him that created him"* (Col. 3:10).

- *"Not by works of righteousness which we have done, but according to his mercy he saved us, by the washing of regeneration, and renewing of the Holy Ghost"* (Titus 3:5).

Paul was a great psychologist because he knew the problem with people is in the way they think. If they would change their thinking to fit what God is doing, they would be believers who function as God intended for them to function on earth.

Vanity of the Mind
Your nature has already been exchanged. You had a sin-nature, and it has been exchanged for the God-

nature that is now in you. You now have the ability as a believer to be everything God intended you to be. This ability is resident in you right now. It is not coming or going to be; you took on the God-nature the moment you had the exchange of natures. Therefore, you have everything you need. To not think in this manner is what I call "vanity of the mind."

Paul declared, *"That ye henceforth walk not as other Gentiles walk, in the vanity of their mind"* (Eph. 4:17). Four things bring about the vanity of the mind. Paul tells us the first one in Ephesians 4:18: *"Having the understanding darkened."* We have so much junk in our minds that if God hollered at us, we would say, *Let me pray about that.* To begin with, we are loaded down with doctrines we don't need and which keep us tied in knots. In the Christ-life, it is not a question of what you believe; the question is in whom do you believe? Life does not come from what you believe. Life comes from the person in whom you believe.

We are also loaded down with religious church work. Everything you can imagine here loads us down, including ballgames, seminars, marriage counseling, and the like. Our mind is so bogged down that we just cannot think clearly. All during this time, we have Christ in us and don't know it. We act as though He is not our life, our victory, our peace, or our power. We are doing our best to carry this load ourselves. Our minds are so bogged down with the weight that our understanding is darkened with a host of things no longer applicable to who we are.

As a result of the mind being darkened, the second thing Paul said in verse 18 is, *"being alienated from the life of God."* We only come in contact with His life when we are in a severe crisis. Otherwise, it is our life, and we do as we please whenever we want. We are alienated from His life because we don't understand it.

You can be alienated from the life in you by the way you think. Until your mind is given to Christ, you are doing your own thing. Paul had a message on how to handle this condition. Paul decided he was not going to let anything defeat him in this world, for it did not matter if he lived or died. He said to die is victory! It was okay to live, as he might be able to help someone, but to die was gain (Phil. 1:21).

Paul depended on the life that was in him. The life that is in you is eternal life; therefore, the real you is an eternal being who is eternally alive right now. Paul said we needed to get this fixed in our minds. I must decide I don't want to be alienated from this life that is in me. If Christ lives in me and that is really where my life is, I want to know it. Now we are talking about the mind.

When God created you in your mother's womb, He created you with the potential to be operated by Christ in you. All human beings are created by God to operate with Christ in them. If they never come to know Christ, their life is never completed. If you thought about that, wouldn't you want to spend every moment possible learning this Christ who is in you? You can choose to be alienated from that life in you, if that is what you want. You can have Christ in you and never recognize Him, never honor Him, never turn to Him, and keep reaching outside of yourself, trying to find another hope, another blessing, another truth. If you turn to Christ in you and give Him your mind, you will begin to function as God created you. That was His purpose and plan.

Let's continue in Ephesians 4:18 with the third cause of vanity of the mind. Paul did not beat around the bush. He said we are ignorant; we have not allowed our minds to take on the truth and the understanding that God intended. If you want to grow in your relationship with God, you will have to spend some time letting the Holy Spirit teach you as you read the Scriptures, listen to tapes, read articles and books dealing with the Christ-life. The Holy Spirit is given solely to your soulish area and does not work in a vacuum. We need Him because we don't function properly as Christians with our old, un-renewed mind.

Paul's fourth reason for vanity of the mind is *"because of the blindness of their hearts."* The heart is where the love affair is. Verse 18 is really connected to verse 20 where he said, *"But ye have not so learned Christ."* This verse focuses on a major problem—we have a love affair everywhere except with Christ in us. We love God. We love our church. We love other believers. We love our families. We love God's Word. We love to sing and pray to God. But we seldom have a love affair with the Christ within us. The only Christ on earth that you can come to know and to fix in your mind is the one who is in you. That is where your love affair should be. Remember, love is an act of the mind, a decision, a choice.

What was the *"blindness of their heart"* of which Paul spoke? Christian people look everywhere for Christ except in themselves. Vanity of the mind separates you from the Christ in you. Many songs you sing, by their words, separate us from Christ, such as "Cast me not away from thy presence, Oh Lord," and "Take not Thy Holy Spirit from me." The teaching of many radio preachers will separate you from the Christ who is in you by saying, for example, *I ask you, God, to reach out and touch these believers in their trials.* In most church buildings, a state of separation from Christ will be expressed because the preacher will eventually say, *If you don't come to our church service every Sunday, you are not a good Christian.* That statement separates you from Christ because it does not matter whether you go to a church building or not, the truth is you are in a non-separated state from Christ in you. I don't want to be separated from Him in my thinking any longer. I am beginning to fashion a love affair with Him, and I am coming to the place where I see He is my real life, my only life. I am not Jesus Christ, but as His Spirit comes through me, that is the real me because He completes my creation the way God made me. My love must return to Him. Therefore, you have to change your vocabulary. You have to sing to Christ who is within you because He is the strongest message in the New Testament. Even Jesus said, *"I am the vine, ye are the branches"* (John 15:5). You get your strength from the vine. The fruit comes from the vine. The power comes from the vine. We fall in love with the Christ who is in us.

Ephesians 4:20 is also important: *"But ye have not so learned Christ."* I believe you learn Christ by how you express Him. I learn Christ by my failures, by my shortcomings, by my separated state from Him in my mind when I do the things that are contrary to what I know of Him.

What Do I Do?

So what do I do? To answer this question, I am going to introduce you to what I call Paul's 13 I-statements in Philippians 3. These will show you what the "I" does. What do I do now that I am saved and I am a Christian? Starting at verse 7:

> *But what things were gain to me, those I counted loss for Christ. Yea doubtless, and I count all things but loss for the excellency of the knowledge of Christ Jesus my Lord: for whom I have suffered the loss of all things, and do count them but dung, that I may win Christ.*

I suffered the loss. God did not come and take it away. I suffered the loss of it by giving it up. I count all things but dung that I may win Christ. The best translation for the Greek word *win* is "to know," so it would read, *"that I may* [know] *Christ."*

> *And be found in him, not having mine own righteousness, which is of the law, but that which is through the faith of Christ, the righteousness which is of God by faith: that I may know him, and the power of his resurrection, and the fellowship of his sufferings, being made conformable unto his death, if by any means I might attain unto the resurrection of the dead. Not as though I had already attained, either were already perfect: but I follow after, if that I may apprehend that for which also I am apprehended of Christ Jesus. Brethren, I count not myself to have apprehended: but this one thing I do, forgetting those things which are behind, and reaching forth unto those things which are before, I press toward the mark for the prize of the high calling of God in Christ Jesus.* (Phil. 3:7–14)

Four of the "I" expressions mentioned in verses 7 and 8 have to do with consecration, and nine of them in verses 9 through 14 have to do with commitment. The difference between consecration and commitment is that consecration is where the Holy Spirit is doing a work; commitment is where you make up your mind to do something, or you feel led of God to do something. Paul stated in verse 13, *I don't know everything there is to know, "but this one thing I do," I forget those things that are behind.* Forgetting those things that are behind is the greatest psychological statement in the whole Bible. If we could just forget, life would be so much simpler for us. I used to tell people who were in counseling to forget the past and move on. Usually they responded that they could not forget. To forget does not mean that it goes away; it is just that you don't remember. The opposite of forgetting is remembering. The past is still there, but I forget it! In fact, I must have something trigger it in me—such as when my memory is stirred by something I see on television or by something someone says—for me to remember what happened 50 or 60 years ago. By forgetting the things that are behind, you can now focus on who and what you are in Christ. Paul's writings reveal the greatest mind change a human being has to make.

Let us move now to Romans 6:3, which starts with the word *know*. Paul has four great things you need to know from this sixth chapter. The first is in verse 3:

> *Know ye not, that so many of us as were bap-*
> *tized into Jesus Christ were baptized into his*
> *death? Therefore we are buried with him by*
> *baptism into death: that like as Christ was*
> *raised up from the dead by the glory of the Fa-*
> *ther, even so we also should walk in newness of*
> *life. For if we have been planted together in the*
> *likeness of his death, we shall be also in the*
> *likeness of his resurrection.*

The two things you need to keep in mind are: first, that we were in Him in His death, burial, and resurrection; and second, that Paul is not talking about water baptism. We read that we were planted together; we were buried with Him—not He for me, and not me alone.

Verse 3 is used every time someone is baptized in water, and it is taught that by the baptismal water immersion we are buried with Christ. That is not what this Scripture is talking about at all. If I am buried with Him when He was buried in Jerusalem, and if I died with Him on the cross and also was resurrected with Him on Easter Sunday morning, then how in the world can some manmade church doctrine be more effective than something God did? I am not objecting to water baptism, but my burial took place when Jesus went into the grave because I was with Him. I was there when Joseph of Arimathaea and Nicodemus put Him in that newly-hewn tomb. I came out with Him when He came out of that tomb on the resurrection morning. I cannot go along with the understanding that you are not really saved until you get water baptized. Before the crucifixion, people participated in the baptism of John the Baptist. Paul did not say we are baptized into water but baptized into Christ, *"Know ye not, that so many of us as were baptized into Jesus Christ"* (Rom. 6:3). When the Holy Spirit revealed Christ in him (Gal. 1:15–16), Paul knew he was no longer an Israelite and was not being baptized into Moses' Law. Accordingly, Jesus prayed in John 17:21, *"As thou, Father, art in me, and I in thee, that they also may be one in us."* Paul could now see that Christ was in him and that Christ is also in us. *"For by one Spirit are we all baptized into one body, whether we be Jews or Gentiles, whether we be bond or free; and have been all made to drink into one Spirit"* (1 Cor. 12:13). There is no more baptism as taught by John the Baptist. That took a colossal mind change for Paul. That is like taking a Church of Christ believer and telling him there is no more water baptism according to the final gospel.

Romans 6:3 further states that we were baptized into His death. When He died, I died. How does this affect the message? You can no longer say you have this little problem or habit you cannot overcome. You are as dead to God as Jesus was on the cross. Paul said we are dead to sin. If a drunkard says he is a Christian but cannot quit drinking, I say, *Friend, you are dead to that.* You may tell me, *Well, I have tried, and everyone has prayed for me, and I cannot get help.* Just remember that you are as dead to it as He was dead on the cross. Don't look at yourself, look at Him. When you look in the mirror and say, *Boy, I will never make it,* you are right. Instead, when you look in the mirror you should say, *I see Jesus in me;* then you will make it. You are dead to sin and dead to the law.

Knowing Nothing but
Jesus Christ and Him Crucified

Let us go to another verse of Scripture, 1 Corinthians 2:2. *"For I determined not to know any thing among you, save Jesus Christ, and Him crucified."* I think of what a tremendous mind change came to Paul to be able to say that he was determined to know nothing except Jesus Christ and Him crucified. I get my understanding for spontaneous living from that Scripture. Once you give your mind to Christ, He will spontaneously come out of you. Spontaneous living comes from determining to know nothing except Christ and Him crucified. Paul's past was no longer his life— Christ became his life. If Christ wants to use the things of the past, He can do it. However, Paul said he was determined not to know his past. For this Scripture to be rightly divided, Paul put *"and him crucified"* into the verse. If he had not put this phrase in, it would have been contrary to 2 Corinthians 5:16, *"Yea, though we have known Christ after the flesh, yet now henceforth know we him no more."* The only Christ Paul wanted to know was Christ crucified, and it should be that way with us. Most of us know all about Jesus of Nazareth, but what we need to know is that our life is in Christ crucified. Paul knew many things, but he set everything aside. He suffered the loss of it all for the excellency of this knowledge of Christ in him. We need to ask if we have done that. Has any of that worked in us?

First Corinthians 2:2 says, *"For I determined not to know any thing among you, save Jesus Christ, and him crucified."* This is the criterion for my life, by which I gauge myself. Since I have known this verse, I have wanted to know nothing but Jesus Christ and Him crucified. I began to see that the more I knew Christ, the more Christ could come through everything God had created me to be. Some time ago, a woman gave one of my books to her preacher. After reading the book, her preacher said I was not balanced because all I knew was Christ. That is quite correct, as all I want to know is Christ! Look at everything Paul knew, but he still was able to say, *I am determined to know nothing but Christ.* If you will do the same, then Christ can use everything you are. He will come out of you as you are, and that is what He wants.

Forgiveness in the Person of Christ

Go to 2 Corinthians 2:10, *"To whom ye forgive any thing, I forgive also: for if I forgave any thing, to whom I forgave it, for your sakes forgave I it in the person of Christ."* Paul did not beat around the bush. He did not say the Spirit of the Lord came upon me and I forgave. He said, *I forgive in the person of Christ.* Someone will say, *Well, we have our own personality; Jesus does not give us personality.* Yes, He does! He uses my personality, but His personality overwhelms mine and comes through my personality. I love a little, but He loves a lot. I love certain ways, but He loves other ways. He comes through what I am, but bigger, expanded, and greater is His person. When Paul said, *"Forgave I it in the person of Christ,"* he said it is not in me to forgive, it is not in me to love, it is Christ who loves through me. It is not in me to be patient; it is Christ who is my patience. It is Christ who is the forgiver. The hardest thing most Christians have to do is to forgive. It is hard for them to forgive one who is in a different doctrine. Paul said, *I cannot forgive of myself, so I forgive in the person of Christ.*

We don't want to forgive because to do so is an attack on our identity. Many marriages could be saved if we would forgive. We all do wrong and make mistakes. Many marriages end in divorce because the individuals involved cannot stand an attack on or a loss of identity. Someone might say, *Well, I cannot live with my spouse any more. We just don't agree, and we don't have anything in common.* This person perceives an attack on his or her identity. However, love is a decision, and you make up your mind to love someone. That same person might have said in the past, *Well, God put it in me to love that person.* I have heard people say a lot of things God told them to do that changed later, but you don't change true love. True love is a mind thing, a decision, because that fits the Christ in you. To love regardless and unconditionally fits this Christ. You can forgive in the person of Christ.

In 2 Corinthians 3:5, we read, *"Not that we are sufficient of ourselves to think any thing as of ourselves; but our sufficiency is of God."* It takes a real mind change to come to this position. Nine times out of 10, when you say, "I can do it," you are depending upon yourself. If you can change that statement to, *My sufficiency is of the Christ that is in me,* God might use all the things you said you could do within yourself. But if you don't let Him do it, then it is not real. How much better it is in your own mind to think, *I can do nothing aside from Christ.* Look at all the power Jesus had, but He said, *I do nothing except what my heavenly Father wants done.* So it must be with us. This mind change is giving your mind to the Christ in you. You can do all things because Christ is your sufficiency.

I interact with many people who are dying, and many of them believe in divine healing. They believe God should have healed them. They have been prayed for and ministered to by everyone, and they are down in the dumps as to why God does not heal them. They tell me they know God can heal them, but no one can get hold of God these days. If we talk like that, we have forgotten that Christ is our sufficiency. I tell these people, *If you keep looking for a healer from outside, for someone to pray a prayer of faith, for someone who has power, what have you said about the Christ who is in you? He is your sufficiency, not something on the outside.* Death is not bad, if Christ is your all. Paul said it did not matter if he lived or if he died because he had come to the place where Christ was sufficient. If He is sufficient whether I live or die, He is also sufficient whether I am sick or well. Change your thinking from the outer to the inner where Christ is in you.

Look at Philippians 4:13, *"I can do all things through Christ which strengtheneth me."* What that verse really says in the original is, *"I do all things through Christ who is my strength."* As it appears in the King James Bible, it seems to lead you to believe that you can do all things if He strengthens you, but it really says *because He strengthens you!* Your strength, the only strength you have, is Christ in you. He is your only life; you do not have another life. There is not a you and a Him. *"But he that is joined unto the Lord is one spirit"* (1 Cor. 6:17). To God you are one. He does not *give* you strength; He *is* your strength. With this mind set, we really begin to live the Christian life. I am a Christian, a Christ-person. I do all things through His strength. Paul came to the understanding that his strength was the Lord, and it is through his teaching on the mind that we learn this truth as well.

Chapter 6
Review Questions

1. It has been said that knowing you are in Christ can change your prayer life. After having a revelation of Christ being in you, how do you feel about praying to be removed from all uncomfortable situations in this life?

2. Explain why your spirit is perfect.

3. When the Bible talks about Christian growth and having Christ formed in you, where and how does this growth occur?

4. If another Christian tells you they want to have more of God in them, how would you respond?

5. How has knowing nothing but Jesus Christ and Him crucified changed your Christian walk?

6. How is it that a Christian is capable of forgiving others regardless of what the circumstances may be?

Now while Paul waited for them at Athens, his spirit was stirred in him, when he saw the city wholly given to idolatry ... And they took him, and brought him unto Areopagus, saying, May we know what this new doctrine, whereof thou speakest, is? ... Then Paul stood in the midst of Mars' hill, and said, Ye men of Athens, I perceive that in all things ye are too superstitious. For as I passed by, and beheld your devotions, I found an altar with this inscription, TO THE UNKNOWN GOD. (Acts 17:16–28)

CHAPTER 7
Paul and Religion

Introduction

The in-Christ message in the Scriptures is the great "mystery" defined in Colossians 1:26–27 as *"Christ in you, the hope of glory."* The Apostle Paul deals with this mystery in everything he touches. The mystery is a motivating factor, an abounding joy in all of Paul's writings. Paul had the awesome responsibility of denying religion its place in his life for the knowledge that Christ was in him as his life.

Remember, when we speak of religion, we are not talking about spiritual beliefs in general, as the world defines *religion.* When I talk of *religion,* I am referring to the teaching of self-effort to earn God's approval or the effort of mankind to gain salvation or righteousness on his own, apart from Christ. This definition of *religion* stands in stark contrast to the gospel of grace, which is God's acceptance of man based only on His Son's sacrifice and the Spirit of His Son in the human who accepts this free, unmerited gift.

Paul is the first one in God's administration who moved from religious effort to the in-Christ position. You have probably never had the experience of reading the Bible in this manner. If not, you have missed something very important because that is exactly what we are all doing in our walk with God. We are moving from a religious position to an in-Christ position in our understanding. I would like to tell you that being in Christ is just an addition to religion, but it is not. From my viewpoint, it is not even a part of religion.

Religion and Its Effects

Religion was a great factor in Paul's life, and the Scriptures are permeated with religion. Israel, in their Babylonian captivity, learned about false religion. To this day, Israel has never been free of that Babylonian contamination. Religion was the culprit that prevented Israel from accepting her Messiah. Religion, in harmony with the Roman Empire, nailed Jesus to the cross. It was religion that kept the early Church from moving into the deeper things of God, especially into Paul's message. Finally, it was religion, the circumcision branch of the Church of Jerusalem that set out to kill the Apostle Paul. Religion has been a devastating force throughout the Scriptures.

In our time, we throw the term *religion* around in a different manner. James 1:27 refers to pure and undefiled religion, of which there is no such thing. I say this in light of what I see to be the definition of *religion,* anything a human being does within himself to please God, contrasted with acknowledging Christ as believers' life and allowing Christ within to live through the believer. It was never God's intention that human beings serve Him within themselves.

When you came into this world, you had a sin-nature. The sin-nature came directly from Satan, and you were motivated and stirred by that nature and did not even know it. That is why Jesus said, *"Ye must be born again"* (John 3:7), because you needed a new nature. The new nature is the God-nature, Christ in you. The God-nature is to fulfill who you are. From the time of Adam's sin onward, every human being who comes into this world is never a self-unto-self. He is either a self guided by the Satan-nature, or he is a self guided by Christ.

Paul's Great Revelation

Apostle Paul was steeped in religion. However, he was saved on the road to Damascus, and called by Jesus to suffer for Him. Three years later, he was led by the Spirit to the Arabian Desert where, in Galatians 1:15–16, he said, *"But when it pleased God, who separated me from my mother's womb, and called me by his grace, to reveal His Son in me."* He received the most awesome information God has ever given to a human being. The greatest thing that ever happened, aside from the Cross, was God telling Apostle Paul that another person lived in him. What a new understanding that is, and how contrary it is to human understanding, contrary to science, religion, and anything that has ever been known on this earth. However, the Church has not interpreted these Scriptures that way. I can hear preachers saying now, *Well, brother Paul went out into the desert, and he felt the presence of the Lord. Jesus was right there with him.* That is not what happened at all. Religion has watered down, twisted, turned, and changed the events that are plainly written in the Scriptures so that we don't know what God really said any more. You can buy commentary books, and they will tiptoe around the subject and never explain it clearly. The Greek scholars often disagree as to what a subject means; therefore, it is left to the believer by the power of the Holy Spirit to come to a revelation. Paul prays that you might have a revelation of this Christ in you. When God said He put His Son in you, He is not just talking about a spirit, or the presence of God, or a grand and glorious experience. He is talking about another person, Christ, occupying the vessel of the human being. He is talking about something that is a direct opposite to Satan being our nature. This is very real and very potent.

The In-Christ Understanding

You were born into this world with a nature that is contrary to your creation. You did awful things, but you thought, *That is who I am.* No one, before they were born again, ever praised the Devil for his nature being in them. No one ever got up in the morning and said, *Oh, Devil, we are going to really have a time today.* We never said things like that! In the same way, the churches of today don't say that about Christ either! God's people today don't run around saying, *Oh, Lord, I thank you that you are in me.* But some of us do see Christ in us, and that is what happened to Paul. Paul saw that another person occupied him, even as the sin-nature had occupied him previously. This means you and I have to pick up Paul's language. Paul never said, *I just have a wonderful blessing knowing the Lord is always with me.* Paul said, *"I am crucified with Christ: nevertheless I live; yet not I, but Christ liveth in me: and the life which I now live in the flesh, I live by the faith of the Son of God"* (Gal. 2:20). In 2 Corinthians 2:10, he said, *"Forgave I it in the person of Christ."* It was never in his attitude or understanding that the truth of Christ in us was just a blessing or a wonderful experience. Those are religious understandings. Religion has taken the truth of being born again and made it so common and ordinary that an individual believer has to spend a lifetime getting hold of the idea that the real "me" is Christ. Religion has fixed us so that we have no concept of who and what we are in Christ.

Paul's Gospel

When we first come into the world, our mind has what I call a horizontal, earthly, or carnal form. The first gospel we hear is also a very carnal gospel. The kingdom message, which Jesus of Nazareth brought to Israel, is a carnal or earthly message. The prophets in the Old Testament taught the kingdom message. The mind of man became saturated with what I call horizontal influence and knowledge. When the final gospel was given to the Apostle Paul, we see that this message was not an earthly message, but it was another message altogether. This new message was vertical or heavenly. The born-again believer is no longer earthly motivated; we are heavenly motivated. Ephesians 2:6 states clearly, *"And hath raised us up together, and made us sit together in heavenly places in Christ Jesus."* Ephesians 1:3 also says, *"Who hath blessed us with all spiritual blessings in heavenly places in Christ."* It was God's intention that we have this radical change from an earthly gospel, which is horizontal, to a heavenly gospel, which is vertical. Sad to say, that kind of change does not come instantly because the mind of the Christian is confused by religion commingling the two gospels. The believer is born again, and in God's sight seated in heavenly places. But the Christian is so mixed up between what is his as a spirit being who belongs in the Father's house and what belongs to an earthly being trying to live on earth. He does not really know who he is. Religion has put us in this sad condition, and we don't know who we are in Christ. A believer may identify himself by saying, *I go to a Baptist church.* Or, perhaps he will say to you, *Well, where do you go to church?* That helps to identify you. We have become so mixed up between the earthly and the heavenly by this commingling that we don't know who we are.

Our Identity

The word *identity* is an important word as we study Paul's epistles. Why is a person confused? He has become confused because he is searching. Religion traps us in a false identity. A person who really wants to know who he is goes from one place to another. A man who had just come out of the Worldwide Church of God came into my office one time. You may know that they had a great organization, but the entire thing fell apart because of law. This man said someone handed him one of our *Life in the Son* magazines, and he was entranced by what was being said in it. He came by the office to see if he could get more literature and to find out more about the message. You must understand that the Worldwide Church of God was a very legalistic work.

He mentioned to me that in order to join their church, he had to send in his financial statement and tax returns so the church could analyze them and tell him how much money to give to the organization. He knew that was not of the Lord and said, "But you get trapped in these things because you are looking for something to belong to, to be a part of and identify with." That is religion at work. Many other things the organization said sounded good, so he went along with it. He also related how he had started out in a Catholic church and discovered some problems there, so he went over to the Baptist church and was saved. After attending the Baptist church for a little while, he was watching some television preachers and decided to go where there was a bit more life than in the Baptist church. So a Charismatic or Pentecostal-type church followed, and from there he ended up in the Worldwide Church of God. He finally came to the point where he felt he had to do some thinking of his own because no one else seemed to be doing any. Those in the churches would tell him what to do. I think he was correct in his analysis. Those organizations just tell you what to do to be one of them. So he was searching once again.

This man had the same problem most of us have had: he left Christ out of his life. We have tried to live for Christ, but we did not know that He was our life and that He was the one to live it, not us. I think this has been a pattern with many of us. We were seeking an identity, so we started out as one thing and then moved to another thing, and then on to another. The church world calls searching people "of no account" because, to them, we never settle down. Nevertheless, we had a right to move on. We always have a right to move on. If you don't like what I say, move on to something else. If we are not careful, we can get trapped in a false identity, which is primarily what religion offers. I hope believers never run around saying they are a "Christ-lifer." I hope you don't allow those tags to be put on you because, most of all, you are a Christian. You are a Christ-person. Just leave it at that.

When someone asks you where you go to church, what they are really doing is trying to get you to identify yourself as to who you are. If you just tell them you are a Christian, that will upset them. Our only identity is Christ in us. Time and again the Apostle Paul dealt with the religion of false identity. He said he no longer lived and he reckoned himself dead. By these statements, he was trying to get rid of anything and everything that kept him from his proper identity. It does not matter where I go or what I believe because that has nothing to do with my identity or who I really am. We get our identity from in whom we believe.

Where Is Our Security?

A second thing Paul dealt with constantly with regard to religion was security. Most people don't feel secure unless they think they have a religion that fits them and they have all the doctrines figured out in their mind. Everyone ends up with a different form of security. The Catholic Church says once you join their church you are a Catholic for life, and that gives you security. Some churches say once you join their church you are eternally secure. There are others who teach once you are in grace, you are always in grace. In the Christ-life we are secure, but our security is not just because of a collection of Scriptures. Eternal security in religion is a collection of Scriptures proving that those who are saved cannot be lost. I refuse to argue eternal security because it is true. I am only secure because Christ lives in me and He is bigger than a collection of Scriptures. Believing in the right collection of Scriptures is not my security. I may not even know all the right Scriptures, but I am secure because when God sees me, He sees His Son in me. My security is my rebirthing, which is the Father's incorruptible seed, Christ, in me. Everyone is looking for security, but you have to be careful because you will receive a false security in religion. You will not have a false security if you know Christ in you is your all.

You will not come to a proper identity or a proper understanding of your security until you do something about the impact of religion in your life. In the Scriptures, we read about a man steeped in many religious ideas who went into the Arabian Desert. He had just about everything religion could offer. Out in the desert, God spoke to him and said, *I accept nothing you have been. I accept nothing you have done. I don't accept who you think you are. I now reveal my Son in you.* Let's say you are in the desert in Arizona, and the Lord reveals Christ in you and says He is your life. When you come out of that desert, what would you say to people? Would you have the courage to say God revealed His Son in you to be your life?

Most in the church world have missed what happened to Paul. Very few writers have ever written books that deal with the subject of what happened to Paul in the Arabian Desert. I have spent well over 30 years trying to find literature that would talk about the in-Christ position for believers. How could writers have missed it? Paul did not miss it. Paul took it to heart. He said, *If another person lives in me, then everything about me has to change.* He dealt with what he believed because what he believed made him who he was.

Recall from chapter 6 that we discussed how Paul had to deal with the false identity he had from religion. In the third chapter of Philippians, he said he was a Hebrew of Hebrews, meaning he was the best Jew you could be. He was of the tribe of Benjamin, which is the most prized tribe. He was a Pharisee, which is the most religious group. He was a persecutor of anyone who disagreed with Judaism. Most of all, he boasted that he was a keeper of the law and no one could keep the law better than him (Phil. 3:5–6). After he received the knowledge that Christ lived in him, he declared in verse 7, *"What things were gain to me, those I counted loss for Christ."* A better translation would be, *Everything that made me who I was, I suffered the loss of for Christ. I set aside my identity found in my education. I set aside my identity in my natural birthing. I set aside all my training as a lawyer and a rabbi. Everything that was gain to me I counted "loss for the excellency of the knowledge of Christ Jesus my Lord"* (v. 8). *I made it but dung or fertilizer.* I know believers who have not yet suffered the loss of their family. I am not saying you are to physically or relationally cease your communication with them, but I am saying they no longer are your identity in your thinking. By this we suffer the loss of the power and the pull they have on us because we now have a new family. Jews would kill people who disagreed with them, let alone someone who was a Jew and renounced it. Paul had done that. The deep root of religion has twisted who we think we are. You have to suffer the loss of that to live as a bona fide Christian because the new life supersedes and overwhelms all that. That old identity cannot be there any more if you are in Christ. Paul suffered the loss of it for a different security and a different identity, and you can do the same.

In religion, we continue to live as believers without Christ as our life. Religion is when you think you can do it. The Scriptures are quite clear that you can do nothing. If you are born again and the Satan-nature is gone, then whatever you do is as a self in union with the Christ who is in you. Anything else is a reversion back to your old way of thinking.

What Paul Did with the Message
    I would like to read and comment on some Scriptures to show you how Paul could not be separated

from the in-Christ truth. Go back to the point where Paul came out of the Arabian Desert after God told him another person lived in him, which was contrary to anything that had ever been said in the history of civilization. What would Paul do with this information? If he spoke of this in front of the Jews, they would laugh at him. If he went to believers in other churches, the Christian churches of the day, they would laugh at him. Paul decided to tell people that Jesus had returned to earth and that He lived in them; Jesus had returned to this earth as Paul. Well, that would blow their minds and definitely upset them. What great courage and valor he showed in stating it exactly as it was.

I think of my preacher friends today who say they believe the in-Christ message, yet when I ask them why they don't preach it, they tell me they have to be careful. The Apostle Paul was never careful; he told the truth as it was revealed to him. It is possible to take a truth and tiptoe around it in such a way that it becomes a lie. Religion has a tendency to do this. If everything has to do with being in Christ, then how could Paul write anything and ignore the fact that we are in Christ?

Some preachers tell me I am not balanced because all I talk about is Christ in the believer. They think I should talk about being a good Christian, a good steward, good mothers, good daddies, good husbands, good wives, good this and good that. As you read Paul, you see he gave very little time for that because he understood that having the knowledge that Christ lives in you overwhelms and takes care of all the concerns of life.

Using a King James Bible, I am going to ask you to mark the words *in whom* in Colossians 2:3. In verse 5 of that chapter, mark *in Christ*. In verse 6, mark *in Him*. In verse 7, mark *in Him*. In verse 9, mark *in Him*. In verse 10, mark *in Him*. In verse 11, mark *in whom*.

By doing this, you can see that Paul could not speak without the in-Christ message prevailing. Paul didn't have a theme that didn't flow out of Christ. He didn't have an idea that did not come from Christ. There is not a thing in existence that is separated from the in-Christ message. You must see this great truth! Paul wrote in the manner of *in Christ, in Him,* and *in whom* at least 146 times in his epistles. Why? Paul was overwhelmed with this understanding. This is not just another bit of religion or theology. It is life—the life is in the Son, which is the only life there is. He could not get away from that, and neither can you or I.

Religion will pick up many good things to preach and teach; however, religion is set against the message of Christ in us because, if we see Christ in us, we will not need religious effort any more. In defense of itself, religion will keep us from knowing this truth. Most of the new Bible translations eliminate the in-Christ statements. The Amplified Bible is pretty good, as it does not cut out many of them. The Living Bible has cut out almost all the in-Christ statements. This has been done because the understanding of being in Christ is destructive to religion. Religion cannot operate unless it has you doing something. It cannot tolerate the idea that we stand perfect before God because Christ lives in us. Religion says you are perfect before God only if you go to a church meeting, give your money, read your Bible, and pray. You have to work at it really hard, and you cannot have a day off or you will fall. If you fall down, or backslide, you have to repent and come back. In reality, from the moment you were born again, God depended on the seed He placed in you. Religion cannot agree with that because they think people would not come back again. The fear of low attendance often keeps religion from preaching the true gospel that would liberate and set people free.

One of the most powerful teachings we find in the Scriptures on the subject of religion is found in Colossians 2:8, *"Beware lest any man spoil you through philosophy and vain deceit, after the tradition of men, after the rudiments of the world, and not after Christ."* Paul lists a number of things that constitute the antithesis to Christ, and they are all religious. Philosophy, vain deceit, traditions of men, and rudiments of the world (being able to attract the world through what you do) are not really bad things, but none of these are Christ. The point I want to make is that if it is not Christ, it doesn't have life in it.

Someone came to me once and said he had read a most powerful book, but it was not really Christian. It had so many good things in it that we ought to know about. I said to him, "If it is not Christ, it is not life." You must always have that in mind. If someone said to me that he went to a church service where the people were shouting, praising God, seeing miracles and wonderful things happening, I would have to say, *If it is not Christ, it is not life.* You must come to look at things as God looks at them. Christ is your only life. That is what I see in this eighth verse.

Paul said you should beware lest any man spoil you through philosophy. Man's philosophy is the way men put things together. If someone says his preacher preaches good sermons on how to be saved, how to be filled with the Holy Spirit, and how to have a happy marriage, I would ask, *Does he preach that you are in Christ?* If he does not preach Christ in you, then it is philosophy. It is usually at this point that people dislike me. People may say they are preaching the gospel, but you cannot separate Christ from the gospel.

Look at 1 Corinthians 12:13: *"For by one Spirit are we all baptized into one body* [Christ].*"* Multitudes of people are saved yet know nothing about being in

Christ. To be saved without this liberating knowledge is truly the grace of God. Even in the Scriptures, we see there were multitudes saved who did not know what it meant to be in Christ. You can be saved and go to heaven but still not know this truth. When anyone denies you truth, they have made your walk on earth twice as difficult. The blessing of knowing about being in Christ is that you walk without fear. You walk knowing it is not what you do that saves you. You walk knowing that if you did not get a chance to read your Bible this week, if you did not get a chance to pray as you like to, or if you did not get a chance to do any good works, you still stand perfect before God because the birthing is what makes you who you are. You are able to live as God intended you to live and not be under the bondage that there is something you must do to make things in life work. The fact is that I can do nothing to make them work. I can do a lot by expression, but I cannot do anything to make Christ in me any greater. He is in me fully and completely.

I was a Christian for years, and no one told me what it meant to be in Christ. I had been deceived. Religion becomes a form of deception. It deceives you into thinking you are alright if you keep the rules, follow the doctrine, and do everything you are told to do. You doing anything within yourself is religion to Christ, compared to Him working through you, which is life.

Paul mentions *"the tradition of men"* in Colossians 2:8. Do you know that men's traditions are made upon what men determine to be scriptural? Each one of us has a form of tradition. I met a fellow who said he liked to get up at four o'clock in the morning and read his Bible. I met another fellow who said he liked to stay up late at night. They were opposite in what they did, but they had formed a tradition. If either of these men thinks what he is doing is what saves him, he is deceived. One of them might hear the other talking about getting a blessing by getting up early in the morning. The other one has been doing it late at night, but he decides to try getting up early in the morning. Getting up early does not fit him because he cannot necessarily do what someone else does. Tradition is not helpful when you think you have to do something to be who you are. If you think you have to pray a certain way or read your Bible a certain way to be who you are, that is bad for you. What you are doing is not a bad thing; however, it is bad if you are anchoring it to your security by saying that the doing is what makes you who you are. I have a new life, and I am happy with who I am in Christ rather than in what I do.

Colossians 2:12–15 go on to say,

Through the faith of the operation of God [The believer has the faith of God in him, as previously explained.]. ... *And you, being dead in your sins and the uncircumcision of your flesh, hath he quickened together with him, having forgiven you all trespasses; Blotting out the handwriting of ordinances that was against us, which was contrary to us, and took it out of the way, nailing it to his cross; and having spoiled principalities and powers, he made a shew of them openly, triumphing over them in it.*

I want to talk about the words *"contrary to us."* I am contrary to my life in this world. Paul said in this life, of all men, he was most miserable. The world is contrary to who we are in Christ. In verse 14, Paul said ordinances are contrary to us. Ordinances in religion are when someone says you have to do something a certain way in order to be one of us. Instead, we follow what the Christ within is leading us to do and not a system of rules and regulations. Some people like to have rules and legalism, but those are not for you in the Christ-life. If you want ordinances, you will have to get them somewhere else because Christ has set us free to fulfill our lives the way God has created us. Law restrictions cannot be set up because everyone is different. You need to be who God made you to be under His power and glory.

Colossians 2:10 mentions another thing contrary to us, which are principalities. *"And ye are complete in him* [Jesus] *which is the head of all principality and power. "* Jesus is in charge of the Devil. Verse 15 states, *"And having spoiled principalities and powers, he made a shew of them openly, triumphing over them in it* [His cross]. *"* We have many believers today chasing the Devil and talking about deliverance when what they need is to see Christ! It is contrary when someone tells me I am not preaching enough about the Devil. Jesus has already defeated the Devil. As you learn Christ, you will be surprised how little you will see the Devil. I am not telling you he is not real or does not have power; his influence has been nailed to the cross. Christ triumphed over the Devil, and now Christ lives in me. That is good news!

There comes a time when the powers of this world become contrary to me. I am in the world but not of the world. I don't become entangled in the things of the world. The world is not my real home. Jesus did not preach against slavery or Roman occupation, neither did Paul. As a matter of fact, Paul told the slave, Onesimus, to go back to his master.

Many people live under heavy law in their honoring of special days and seasons (Col. 2:16), yet these things were nailed to the cross. One thing that would be contrary to a Christ-life believer would be to say there are special days. We are not bound by special days or holidays. However, we are not under a law that says we cannot celebrate them. This is the freedom we have in Christ.

Chapter 7
Review Questions

1. What problems can you see if a person tries to add the Christ-life understanding onto their religious understandings?

2. If you were asked to describe your identity, how would you respond?

3. Describe what you believe is your security in this life.

4. How would you describe a religious person?

5. What does the statement *if it is not Christ, it is not life* mean to you?

6. What role does the Devil play in your spiritual life?

*And when it was day, certain of the Jews banded togeth-
er, and bound themselves under a curse, saying that they
would neither eat nor drink till they had killed Paul. And
they were more than forty which had made this conspir-
acy ... And when Paul's sister's son heard of their lying
in wait, he ... told Paul ... So he took him, and brought
him to the chief captain ... And he called unto him two
centurions, saying, Make ready two hundred soldiers to
go to Caesarea, and horsemen threescore and ten, and
spearmen two hundred, at the third hour of the night;
And provide them beasts, that they may set Paul on, and
bring him safe unto Felix the governor. (Acts 23:12–24)*

CHAPTER 8
Paul and the Church

Introduction

Two things astonish me about the Apostle Paul. The first is the radical change he made in his life when he discovered he had another person living in him. The second is that Paul's message is so clearly stated in the Scriptures, yet so many people ignore it or don't see it. If Christ in the believer is the only life of the believer God accepts, then everything the believer touches or has anything to do with is going to be determined by the simple knowledge that another person lives in him.

The Church

Among the many things the Apostle Paul saw in a new way was the issue of the Church, the Body of Christ. The focus in this chapter will be distinctly different from the discussion in chapter 7 on religion. In the Christ-life, when we say *Church,* we mean the Body of Christ. When we say *the Church*, we don't mean a building. The building is not the Church—the Church is the people who received Christ, God's children. A brother in Oregon has a reply to people when they ask him where he goes to church. He tells them it depends on where he is standing at any particular time! The Church is you, and there is no such thing as a church building for a bona fide in-Christ believer. In the Scriptures, there were church buildings; but when the in-Christ understanding came, there were no longer buildings that denoted what the Church was and where the Church was located. The Church is made up of the rebirthed believers, each of them being placed (baptized) into Christ.

At least four different churches are mentioned in the New Testament. The first church in our discussion is the church in the wilderness mentioned in Acts 7:38: *"This is he, that was in the church in the wilderness with the angel which spake to him in the mount Sina, and with our fathers: who received the lively oracles to give unto us."* This was Stephen's final message before he was stoned to death. He referred to the children of Israel as being the church in the wilderness. Israel was a collection of people, but Israel literally had no church. In the wilderness, Israel was a single group of people with whom God dealt. They are not called a church anywhere in the Old Testament. Stephen was the first to bring up this idea.

Let us look at a second church mentioned in the Scriptures, which we could call the early New Testament church. Paul's message of grace was not known at that time. In Matthew 18:15–17 we read,

> *Moreover if thy brother shall trespass against thee, go and tell him his fault between thee and him alone: if he shall hear thee, thou hast gained thy brother. But if he will not hear thee, then take with thee one or two more, that in the mouth of two or three witnesses every word may be established. And if he shall neglect to hear them, tell it unto the church: but if he neglect to hear the church, let him be unto thee as an heathen man and a publican.*

I call this a New Testament church because Jesus taught and ministered in this church. This New Testament church is a progression from the church in the wilderness. You will note in the reading of these previous verses, that the content is based on law. It was a church still preaching Old Testament judgments with no recognition of the Cross. Obviously, this was a Judaistic church. This is one of the few times the term

church is used in what we call "the kingdom message."
Jesus said this man was to be put out of the church;
therefore, you can see clearly that these Scriptures
cannot be used in grace. What trouble we get into by
not rightly dividing the Word of Truth! The very idea
is contrary to the New Testament grace church of the
in-Christ believer.

Prior to Paul talking about the Body of Christ (the
Church), it is important to understand that there were
two different early churches in the New Testament, both
of them started by and drawn from the ministry of Jesus.
Also, you need to see that the ministry of Jesus is two-
fold. One of His ministries was that of the circumcision
rites, which constitutes the continuation of the church in
the wilderness. This is the church of the circumcision,
which Peter continued to perpetuate even after Pentecost (Gal. 2:7–8). Some form of this church still exists
today—those preaching "the gospel of circumcision,"
which is the law or what I call "doer religion," and bits
and pieces of the kingdom message.

The other early New Testament church was the
Pentecostal church. This church perpetuated the ministry of Jesus of Nazareth, incorporating circumcision,
signs, wonders, and miracles. This church was the final tribute to the kingdom message and was, in time,
overwhelmed by Paul's message of grace. It was the
"outer church," the church dedicated to proving God
by the outer manifestation of works. In contrast, this
church, in time, was to give way to the "inner
church," believers who knew they were in Christ.

The fourth church in the New Testament is the
grace church of the uncircumcision. It is to be plainly
noted that these three New Testament churches—the
circumcision church, the early Pentecostal church, and
Paul's church of grace and uncircumcision—were all
started by Jesus. Since all three have different doctrines

that cannot be combined to constitute truth for today, a believer must learn to rightly divide the Truth to know what must be believed. Bible scholars seem to have a difficult time separating these churches, but a close study of the Scriptures themselves is ample evidence that the grace church Christ initiated by Paul is the last Church giving forth the final message to the world before our home-going. This grace church started on the Day of Pentecost when the Holy Spirit came to create a new body on earth, the Body of Christ. His mission was to place every believing soul into Christ. That He did, and He still does so today. It is Christ alive on this earth again by His many-membered Body. The uncircumcision church is referred to in Ephesians 1:22–23, *"And hath put all things under his feet, and gave him to be the head over all things to the church, which is his body, the fullness of Him that filleth all in all."*

Since most Bible scholars have great difficulty separating these churches, I want to point out that Christ gave us the New Testament church (the kingdom church) because that was one of His main purposes for coming to this earth. Therefore, primarily, Christ came to this earth to establish the kingdom and not to give us the Body of Christ Church.

In Matthew chapter 12 (Matthew is the strongest historical record of the kingdom message.), we have two statements that tell us Jesus knew they were going to kill Him (Matt. 12:15, 25). In Matthew 13, we have what we call the "parabolic ministry," where Jesus begins to lay out the parables. Most of the parables have to do with the future state of Israel. It is obvious that the state of Israel, at that time, was one of confusion and her eyes were blinded, which resulted in her rejecting the message Jesus brought in the Gospels. Since Jesus was also dedicated to God's eternal plan (that of birthing His own offspring), He begins what I call the "bridge ministry." He begins to build a bridge from law over to grace. This bridge is most prevalent in the Gospel of John.

The Gospel Bridge of John

John wrote his gospel at least 25 years after Paul's death, and he was able to distinctly portray the bridge. He did not give us the full gospel of uncircumcision— the gospel of grace—but he did give us a bridge to it. As an example, we make much out of John speaking in his epistle about us being in Christ, using words such as *"If ye abide in me, and my words abide in you, ye shall ask what ye will, and it shall be done unto you"* (John 15:7). That is a bridge because it has both ideas in it. If you are looking to get what you want or earn something, that is the kingdom message. In contrast, abiding or being in Christ is the Body-of-Christ message. John commingles the two ideas because he is reporting the words of Jesus with a new understanding after having spent at least 25 years in Christ. In Matthew 16:13 the Scripture reads, *"When Jesus came into the coasts of Caesarea Philippi, he asked his disciples, saying, Whom do men say that I the Son of man am?"* Until this time, Jesus had been proving His ministry by signs, wonders, and miracles. Jesus is doing an important thing here by moving the disciples from what He *does* to a new understanding of who He *is*. That is also what Paul does in the Body of Christ Church. He moves us from the important things Jesus does to who He is because who Jesus is relates to who we are, and that ties us to the Father. *"That they all may be one; as thou, Father, art in me, and I in thee, that they also may be one in us: that the world may believe that thou has sent me"* (John 17:21). This Scripture is what we are aimed at and where we are headed in Christianity.

I know this is hard on some people who have Pentecostal and Charismatic backgrounds because it leaves you wondering what you are to believe. Jesus, Himself, moved the people to something greater, but most did not catch it. It is the same today. The world would rather see God do something for them than understand who they are in Christ. This is all because of the way we think. Becoming who you are in Christ is far more important than what He does for you. Most people don't realize the knowledge of who they are in Christ is their greatest power. I base my statement on Acts 1:8, *"But ye shall receive power, after that the Holy Ghost is come upon you."* The word *after* tells me it is the teaching of the Holy Spirit, the revelatory ministry of the Holy Spirit, which gives us the ultimate power. I can tell you that you will not get an answer to every prayer you pray or a miracle to every problem in life. You are not going to get a healing to everything that is wrong in your body. What then is the power of the gospel? The power of the gospel is in knowing who you are. That is very different from anything we have heard in the past.

When John the Baptist sent word wondering who Jesus was, Jesus sent back the kingdom message, the early New Testament church message. He said to John in Luke 7:22, *"The blind see, the lame walk, the lepers are cleansed, the deaf hear, the dead are raised."* He talked about His miraculous power so that John would know. John the Baptist did not know Christ as life. He knew the Messiah was a miracle worker, and Jesus was confirming that to him. In Matthew 16, Jesus is moving them from what He can do to who He is. In verses 14–15 we read, *"And they said, Some say that thou art John the Baptist: some, Elias; and others, Jeremias, or one of the prophets. He saith unto them, But whom say ye that I am?"* Jesus is asking a very difficult question, and the fact is they are not able to answer that question within themselves. *"And Simon Peter answered and said, Thou art the Christ, the Son of the living God"* (v. 16). It looked as if Peter had the answer, but Jesus knew better. This is a profound question of Christianity. Who is He? *"And Jesus answered and said unto him, Blessed art thou, Simon Barjona: for flesh and blood hath not revealed it unto thee, but my Father which is in heaven"* (v. 17). Peter knew Jesus as a miracle worker, as the one who walked on water and multiplied the loaves and fishes; however, he did not know Him as the Christ, the Son of the living God, without a revelation. What this tells us, ultimately, is that Christ is only to be known by revelation. The day will come when the dead will be raised and the sick will be healed, but they will not believe in Christ. In fact, in John 12:37 it is stated that, although He performed many miracles, they did not believe. So what God does in the "outer" is going to be eclipsed and overwhelmed by something greater, and that something greater is where we know the Christ-life understanding right now.

This message is reaching people who have become disenchanted in the outer things. If I were Satan, I would get God's people focused on the outer things. I would keep the churches at that level because those churches would only know what Jesus does, not who He is. So Jesus said to Peter, *"Flesh and blood,"* which is to say, *You did not get that understanding from men.* It did not come from scholars. It did not come out of the Old Testament. Where did Peter get this understanding? The Father in heaven revealed it. I have to place great emphasis on this point. You can read this book and any book you choose and never come to know Christ as your life until the Holy Spirit reveals it to you. Man can say truth exists, but no man can give revelatory understanding. I can only say it exists, and that is what teaching and preaching is all about. It is up to the Holy Spirit to reveal it. I get very upset when I hear people using the Holy Spirit to do everything they want while ignoring His greatest ministry of revealing Christ as their life. Whatever you get from the Holy Spirit, if He did not reveal Christ in you, you took a lesser truth. You took the outer thing. You took the earthly thing.

I would suggest you draw a circle around the word *revealed* in Matthew 16:17. You will not understand the true Church of Jesus Christ, the Body of Christ, if you don't see that, on the Day of Pentecost, Jesus returned to believers in a different form.

Two Bodies of Christ

In the Scriptures, Jesus is represented in two different bodies. It is important that you distinguish between these two different bodies. The first body of Jesus was the body Mary gave to Him in Bethlehem. All Mary did was to give Him a body. He would get all of His understanding, His wisdom, and His life from His Father. It is hard to impress upon people today that it is God's plan that the father is the one who gives the nature to the child. The father and the mother join together to give genetics, but only the father can give the nature. In the case of Jesus of Nazareth, God was the Father and Mary was the mother. The first form of Jesus Christ, the Son of God, on this earth was the bodily form given to Him by Mary. That was the body of Christ that walked on water, multiplied the loaves and fishes, and performed the many miracles recorded in the Scriptures. That body eventually bore our sins and that body died. That body in a different form came back on the resurrection morning. The second body is eternal, not given by Mary, but given to Him by the Father. It was an eternal, incorruptible body that Jesus received on the resurrection morning, yet it looks like the body that Mary had given Him (John 20:20). But it is Christ in a different form.

On the Day of Pentecost, that Body of Christ, which is the resurrection body, was made up of many members. The first-joined members were the 120 in the upper room (Acts 1:15), plus 3,000 (Acts 2:41) saved on the Day of Pentecost. Later, another 5,000 (Acts 4:4) were added, and they all became body members. God was making a new body that would be called the Body of Christ. People did not understand what really happened on the Day of Pentecost. They could have seen the fulfillment to Jesus' words in John 14:20 promising they would know Christ in them. Yet, on the Day of Pentecost they mistakenly believed the coming of the Holy Spirit gave them personal power to do the things Jesus of Nazareth had done. For much of my life I dreamed of having power like that, and I have been with groups that taught you could get that kind of power when you received the Holy Spirit. On the Day of Pentecost, the people had all sorts of outer demonstrations, but they did not come to the knowledge that Christ was in them. They thought the Holy Spirit had come to make *them* somebody, to make *them* greater, rather than to reveal Christ who wanted to be their life. They missed the opening day of pure grace because the Pentecost experience was a continuation of the church in the wilderness and the New Testament church of Matthew 18. They missed it because on the Day of Pentecost, Peter got up and preached what Joel had said. The early church was based on Joel's prophecy, which requires the Tribulation period to be fulfilled. It is the kingdom message continued, and it is contrary to the Body of Christ Church. It is important that you see this point.

Joel's Prophecy and Israel

I have preached for many years from the Scripture in Joel 2:28–32:

> *And it shall come to pass afterward, that I will pour out my spirit upon all flesh; and your sons and your daughters shall prophesy, your old*

*men shall dream dreams, your young men shall
see visions: and also upon the servants and upon the handmaids in those days will I pour out
my spirit. And I will show wonders in the heavens and in the earth, blood, and fire, and
pillars of smoke. The sun shall be turned into
darkness, and the moon into blood, before the
great and the terrible day of the Lord come.
And it shall come to pass, that whosoever shall
call on the name of the Lord shall be delivered:
for in mount Zion and in Jerusalem shall be deliverance, as the Lord hath said, and in the
remnant whom the Lord shall call.*

It would amaze you how many times I preached
on this passage and stopped at verse 29. I never read a
thing about the *"wonders in the heavens and in the
earth, blood and fire, and pillars of smoke."* I never
said a thing about *"the sun shall be turned into darkness, and the moon into blood."* These things did not
happen on the Day of Pentecost! And they have not
happened in our day either. These are words speaking
of the Tribulation period. At the end of the Tribulation
period, Israel, in the words of Joel, is going to *"call on
the name of the Lord and shall be delivered."* This is
still an outer work with no change of spirit and no new
life in them. That is not the promise of Pentecost.

When Peter began to preach in Acts 2:14, he said:
"Ye men of Judaea." He was preaching to Israel! The
church spoken of here was not the church that belonged to born-again believers, for Peter did not have
them in focus. What we have, at this point, are believers who have received the Holy Spirit. The Holy Spirit
came on the Day of Pentecost and people were saved.
There was only one kind of salvation at that time, and
it is described in 1 Corinthians 12:13, *"For by one
Spirit are we all baptized into one body."* I believe the
Church started on the Day of Pentecost because that is

the day the Holy Spirit came to baptize believers (place believers) into Christ. What I see lacking on the Day of Pentecost was any revelation to know Christ as the life of the believer. Even though those at Pentecost did not know who they were in Christ, God did His work just the same. They were the first to be born again.

Let me give an example. We live in a day when multitudes of people have had the same experience as happened on the Day of Pentecost over 1,900 years ago. These people are most visible on television and have the greatest religious crowds in America today. These people are no different from the 120 in the upper room on the Day of Pentecost. The latter did not know Christ as their life, and most believers today don't know Christ as their life. They all were placed in Christ, even though they did not know it. I know all brothers and sisters who are saved, regardless of denominational persuasion, are in Christ, just as I am. There is no other kind of salvation. Even though they focus on the outer things and have little or no concept of their in-Christ position, they are born again just like I am. The difference is they don't understand the greatest work of grace available to humans. It is still Christ in us as our only hope of glory (Col. 1:27).

The early New Testament Church, which thrived for a few short years, came to an abrupt end in Acts 7 with the killing of Stephen. If you read the book of Acts closely, you will see that the believers healed the sick, cast out devils, and had miracles on every hand. The Scriptures say over and over that there were great miracles, but after Acts 7, God began to move them into a new understanding. From Acts 7 forward, you never again see things quite like they were. There were a few miracles, just like there are today, but individual ministries began to give way to the Body of Christ ministries. Now Christ was working through individuals. Rather than individuals having the power and gifts to do miracles themselves, it was Christ alive. Around the thirteenth chapter of Acts, the Apostle Paul begins to write his epistles. In 1 Corinthians, Paul moves the believer from the personal gift ministry to something greater. He gives us a deeper understanding of the gifts of the Spirit in 1 Corinthians 12. Paul explains the control of the gifts of the Spirit in 1 Corinthians 14. In chapter 13, the emphasis moves from personal ministry to Body ministry. It must move from self to love. Paul moves the believer to a greater understanding of what is ours in Christ.

The New Body of Christ

The Epistle to the Galatians was written soon after Acts chapter 13. In the time period between Acts 13 and Acts 28, seven of Paul's epistles were written. These epistles are bridge epistles in moving the believer from what Christ can do for you to who He is in you. This moves the people from the early New Testament church of self-ministries to the Body of Christ ministries. Paul recounts, *"But when it pleased God, who separated me from my mother's womb, and called me by His grace, To reveal His Son in me"* (Gal. 1:15–16). This is the first revelation to the new Body of Christ Church. This is the fulfillment of what Jesus said in Matthew 16:18, that His Church would be built on *revelation*. The "rock" is the revelation of Christ in us, the hope of glory, which constitutes the new Body of Christ.

We are each members of Christ's Body, and we have our strength from Christ, who operates as the member we are. No member has strength aside from the Body of Christ. In my study of the Body of Christ, I have come across so many wonderful things that opened up in the Scriptures. All Paul's epistles are difficult to understand and incomplete unless you tie them to the subject of the Body of Christ because that is the platform from which he spoke. He never spoke of his own personal ministry as such because he understood the ministries were resident in the Christ within him and were not his. On one occasion, when he was dealing with the Pentecostals from the early church in Jerusalem, he said, *"I thank my God, I speak with tongues more than ye all"* (1 Cor. 14:18). But he never let that be a thing of power to him. He healed the sick, but that was not his message. He raised the dead on one occasion, but he never gave testimony to it. What he did do was give testimony to his daily walk. He spoke of being shipwrecked three times and knocked down on many occasions. He had a difficult walk. When you read his story, you yourself feel better regardless of where you are in your walk. My understanding from Paul is that every one of us is going to have a hard time because it is the circumstances and situations of life that bring forth the Christ in us.

Moving from Serving God to Knowing God

The Apostle Paul moves the believer from serving God to knowing God. All of us who have been raised in institutional religion believe the greater our service, the more we are a child of God, or the more we earn God's approval, or the more we know God. As I read about some of the greatest people who served God and did great things for God, I see that they actually did not know God as their Father very well. God desires to be known as Father by His children. What father would not want to be known? The Apostle Paul, in the Body of Christ ministry, moves the believer from serving God to knowing God. This doesn't mean we don't serve God anymore! Once a person knows God, you cannot stop him or her from serving God. The more you learn about the Lord, the more you want to tell someone. You eventually get to the place where most of us sense we need to band together and do what we can to share this message with other people.

Moving from Circumcision to Uncircumcision

The Apostle Paul moved us from the gospel of circumcision to the gospel of uncircumcision. I try to make this obvious because it is so predominant in the Scriptures. Many will say there is no such thing as a gospel of circumcision. However, Paul said, *"But contrariwise, when they saw that the gospel of the uncircumcision was committed unto me, as the gospel of the circumcision was unto Peter"* (Gal. 2:7). Some Bible translations are not as clear as the King James Version so perhaps you missed it. For instance, this verse in the New American Standard Bible says, *"Seeing that I had been entrusted with the gospel to the uncircumcised, just as Peter had been to the circumcised."* As you can see, this gives an entirely different meaning to this Scripture.

Paul moved the believer from the gospel of self-effort to God-effort. Someone came to me and said, "I really want to do something for God." I replied, "Well, what is it you think you ought to do?" He responded, "I don't know; why don't you tell me?" I said, "Why don't you forget it?" Do you know why I was so blunt? It is because if it is not a God-effort, it doesn't matter. In grace you do what you feel led of God to do, and it is no one else's business. That is why I don't sit around trying to organize things for others.

Moving to Wholeness in Christ

The Apostle Paul moves the believer from being insecure and wounded to being whole in Christ. We don't realize how beat up we are from religion until we get a taste of living in Christ. I recall a man came to me whose business was going through a real struggle. He said, "I want you to know I could not make it through my business problems if I did not know I was in Christ. I would have given up or would have been destroyed a long time ago." He said his strength is

Christ. He had moved from being insecure and wounded to being whole in Christ.

Moving to What God Tells Us to Do

The Apostle Paul moved us from doing what man says to doing what God says. There are a percentage of people whom I believe cannot stand the liberty of being free. They are like someone who has cancer for which there is a cure but they prefer to be where they are. Everyone who wants to be free in God is going to have to go on by hearing God's voice. That is hard on some people. We don't understand God's voice, and I confess I cannot explain it fully. God's voice is what you know about God in your life and acting on it. You will never know everything the Bible says about God, but God expects you to live what you do know of Him. The best thing James ever said is, *"Therefore to him that knoweth to do good, and doeth it not, to him it is sin"* (James 4:17). God will only judge you on what you know. A person came to me not long ago and said, "I don't know much about God." I replied, "What do you know about Him?" He said, "I know He is big and He is great and you sure better be careful." I told him, "Well, that is what you have to live; be careful."

From Meeting-Oriented to Relationship-Oriented

The Apostle Paul moved us from being meeting-oriented to being relationship-oriented. I used to think big meetings showed forth God. I was an evangelist; and I also pastored churches; and I thought it was only the size of the crowd that showed forth the glory of God. When I began to understand the Christ-life, and did not see large crowds anymore, God really had to deal with me. Finally, I saw that the Apostle Paul was moving the believer away from thinking that success is measured by the great external things God does for us. Now I am relationship-oriented, and I understand that our relationship with others is based upon the fact that we all have the same Father. Therefore, a crowd does not matter.

Changing Our Thinking about Gathering Places

The Apostle Paul moved us from meeting in synagogues and big buildings to home gatherings, or wherever Christians happened to be gathered. People are always saying, "Well, where are your churches?" I respond that it does not matter; it could be in a hotel, a bank, a horse barn, or a room in someone's home. It never entered into Paul's mind that God could be greater by anything that happens on this earth. Human beings can do nothing to make God greater, bigger, more loving, or more powerful. The Apostle Paul moved believers away from thinking that worldly success is spirituality.

Seeing Christ in Others

The Apostle Paul moved believers from looking at others outwardly to seeing Christ in them. We have notable people, by the world's standards, in the Christ-life. We have some fine people, some wealthy and some who hold high positions. If you listen to them speak, you would never know who they are. You would never know what they did. We have doctors who get up to speak in camp meetings, but I cannot remember anyone who talked to us about being a doctor. We have lawyers, and they don't tell us about being lawyers. We have presidents of corporations, but you would never know it. Once you have Christ in you, what can you say about yourself that makes Him greater? What makes Christ more important? Can you do something to make Him bigger or more important? We only want people to talk about being in Christ. We are not organizationally joined together; rather, we are joined together by being birthed by the same Father. Whatever your need is, whatever your problem is, wherever you are in the Lord, Christ in you is the bigger thing. If you are born again, He is already in you. You need to *know* Him, and the more you know Him the more it swallows up everything else in your life.

Chapter 8
Review Questions

1. When you hear the word *church* used in Christian circles:

    a. What can that word mean?

    b. What is your understanding of the word?

2. Explain what the *kingdom church* means.

3. Why should the born-again believer place a greater emphasis on the Gospel of John than on the other three gospels?

4. Explain the difference between knowing Jesus by what He does compared to knowing Jesus by who He is.

5. Acts 1:8 states, *"Ye shall receive power, after that the Holy Ghost is come upon you."* Explain the "power" that is spoken of in this verse.

6. Explain what is meant by "the Body of Christ."

And after certain days, when Felix came with his wife Drusilla, which was a Jewess, he sent for Paul, and heard him concerning the faith in Christ....But after two years Porcius Festus came into Felix' room: and Felix, willing to shew the Jews a pleasure, left Paul bound. (Acts 24:24, 27)

CHAPTER 9
Paul and Meeting Human Needs

Introduction

God chose the Apostle Paul to deliver the most important message He ever entrusted to a human being. The message that another person lived in Paul is recorded by the apostle in Galatians 1:15–16, *"But when it pleased God, who separated me from my mother's womb, and called me by his grace, to reveal his Son in me, that I might preach him among the heathen."* These Scriptures are overlooked most of the time in Christianity. Many Christians spiritualize or allegorize these verses and miss the importance of them. I find writers who speak against Paul because they don't understand him. Many of our brethren in Full Gospel and charismatic churches never preach from Paul because they don't think he had a revelation of faith. When God told Paul that Christ lived in him, it had to be the most abrupt and awesome change that could come to a human being. God told Paul that another person lived in him; and from that moment on, Paul had to identify with that person. He had to cease being a person unto himself and become a person that magnified and manifested Christ. Most theologians never catch that in the Scriptures.

Paul alludes to being in Christ 146 times in his writings. He could not have that information in his mind and not begin to let it work out of him. All born-again Christians have Christ in them, but for the most part they have Him locked up. I often think it is similar to an old man sitting in a rocking chair just waiting for someone to come in and ask advice. They want to keep

Christ on the outside of themselves. They want to use Him when they want Him, but they don't want Him within them to be their life. I think the main reason is because they don't have understanding. They don't know what all this means.

The Change in Paul after His Revelation

If Christ lived in the Apostle Paul, then his ministry of meeting human needs was going to have to change radically. When Paul first met Jesus on the road to Damascus, he was told that he would suffer for Christ's sake. It was about three years later when Paul was in the Arabian Desert that he had a revelation of Christ in him. What did he do during the three years between being saved on the road to Damascus and experiencing the revelation of Christ in him in the Arabian Desert? He was a rabbi. He had abilities to minister as an Israelite, but now he had the message of salvation brought through the death of Christ at the Cross (1 Cor. 2:2). I am sure he went about healing the sick, casting out devils, preaching the Word, and getting into a lot of trouble. Because Paul did not know Christ was in him during that three-year period of time, he ministered just like anyone else would. However, when he received the revelation that Christ was in him, there had to be a drastic change. If Christ was in him, how could he continue his own ministry? How could he continue doing what other preachers were doing who did not know Christ was in them? How could he meet human needs the same as he always did? There had to be a radical change because he saw that if his life was Christ, if Jesus lived in him, there was no need for his own ministry. The ministry of Christ—His words, His love, and His power—must now flow through Paul.

I am sure the preachers in Paul's day patterned themselves after the great people in the Old Testament. Once Paul received a revelation of Christ in him, he could never be like Noah, Abraham, Moses,

David, or any other Biblical character because not one of them had Christ in them! Their ministry was different because everything they did was outer things.

The Outer Things

You must understand something about outer things. With the call of Abraham, God picked Israel to be His chosen people. Israelites are not His sons and daughters. They are not His birthed children. They are a people chosen of God to bring forth the Messiah, whom they later rejected. God only wanted Israel to obey Him. He gave them a law that they could not live, but they tried their level best to keep it. They never did live or keep the law. All the years God dealt with Israel, He was working with them in an outer sense. He never changed their hearts from wickedness to righteousness. There was never a rebirthing. God told Israel to obey and that would make them righteous. This was an earned righteousness, not of pure grace.

It is said that Abraham had faith in God and that action was counted unto him as righteousness. There was no change in heart because it was outer. The outer things are produced by man's effort. In the present church age, we can't do anything to make Christianity work. When the seed, Christ, went into us, we received the righteousness of Christ, and that is what God sees rather than our own efforts. Our own efforts are as filthy rags to God.

All through the Old Testament, it is man's effort producing the outer things. Plagues came upon Egypt because the Egyptians had put the children of Israel in bondage. As wilderness wanderers for 40 years, Israel had signs, wonders, and miracles. Entering into Canaan's land, they had one miracle after another. These outer things caused the people to follow the Lord because of what He did in an outer sense, but there was very little change in their hearts.

The New Covenant in Jeremiah states that when Israel as a nation accepts its Messiah, God will give them a new heart. Since Israel never accepted her Messiah, that promise has never been fulfilled. I hear kingdom preachers today saying if we come to the Lord He will give us a new heart, but that is a promise to Israel, not to the Church. God does not give us a new heart. He gives us a new life altogether. That life is in His Son.

Look at the ministry of Jesus of Nazareth. One miracle after another was used to get Israel's attention. Although Jesus performed all these miracles, it did not change the lives of the people. When Jesus came to the end of His ministry, John 12:37 says, *"But though He had done so many miracles before them, yet they believed not on him."* The signs, wonders, and miracles of Jesus were outer things and never changed the people. We have more outer things in the religious world today than ever before, and television has made that possible. People are doing all sorts of things in meetings before huge crowds. Through all this, I don't see many changed lives; instead I see people who love to be where the outer things are taking place.

Paul's Perspective
The Apostle Paul did not lean on the past because there was no help for him there. He could not talk about the three Hebrew children walking with Jesus in the fiery furnace because Christ was in him now. He could not talk about Noah obeying God and building an ark to please God because Christ was in him now. His great objective in life was the release of Christ from within him. When God revealed that Christ was in Paul, he could not be like anyone else. Paul could get illustrations from Noah, Moses, David, and others in the Old Testament, but he could not go the limit and say we are like them or that we should be like them. Not one of them had the life Paul had, which was

Christ in him. Paul knew that if he was going to meet human need, he could not be like Abraham and be a great man of faith. He could not be like Moses and perform great miracles. He had to be the Christ that was in him, so his outer works decreased and the inner man grew (Eph. 4:13–15).

This same thing is happening today to believers around the world. The great outer things are becoming dim as believers begin to see Christ. Paul expressed that viewpoint in all his writings. Nowhere does he say he is going to give you a great lecture on faith so that you can have faith to do things. Paul said, *"The life which I now live in the flesh I live by the faith of the Son of God"* (Gal. 2:20). I don't put faith in my faith, and I don't put trust in my works. I don't put trust in my prayers. I don't put trust in my past, my gifts, or my ability. *"The life I now live in the flesh I live by the faith of the Son of God."*

Instead of studying how I can get more faith, I am learning the Christ in me so He can come out of me with His great faith and power. That is how you meet human needs. Paul wrote 14 epistles, and he never used the word *heal* one time in his writings. The word *heal* is used over and again in the synoptic Gospels by Jesus of Nazareth. Jesus of Nazareth had a different message than Paul. Jesus of Nazareth's message was that of circumcision. Paul does use the word *healed* in the past tense one time. He uses the expression gift(s) of healing(s) three times, but he never uses the word *heal*. He does not tell us to heal the sick. When Paul received a revelation of Christ in him, the outer things that took place were overwhelmed by this new relationship with Christ in him. This by no means says that healings and miracles did not take place in Paul's ministry. They did. What it means is that something far greater and more important took place. Instead of man using God as He did in the Old Testament, it was now the Christ-life coming through human beings.

To be born again means you have another person in you. You project Christ to the world through your own personality, when you learn Him and give Him your mind. The Apostle Paul was given a commission to bring help to people through a message. The power Paul had was the power of knowing. He knew this message, Christ in you, was so powerful that if people took hold of the fact that Jesus lived in them, their entire lives would be changed.

Paul didn't give us a lecture on how to be healed, how to receive a miracle, or how to obtain greater faith. Jesus of Nazareth taught if you had the faith of a mustard seed whatever you asked for would be given to you. The impossible could be done, including moving trees and mountains. Paul never said anything like that because he had a different message. Paul's message was simply that people don't need outer things. They need to know the Christ who is in them.

When people come to me with their needs and ask me to pray for them, I measure or discern the best I can where they are in the Lord. Many times I pray with them for what they want. If they are strong in the Lord, I usually say, "Your need is not finances, a job, a healing, or salvation for your children. Your need is to know the Christ in you because that is the greatest power you have. It is another way to live Christianity." Paul keeps using terms in his message such as *knowledge*, *wisdom*, *understanding*, and *revelation*. These are key words that have to do with renewing your mind.

Being in a Non-Separated State with Christ

Another little known fact is that Paul prayed at least 33 times in his epistles. You can be reading along in an epistle, going from one verse to the next, without realizing that you have entered into Paul's prayer. In other words, he can be in a narrative and suddenly go into a prayer. Paul understood that as Christ lived in the body given to Him by Mary, Christ now lives in his body given to him by his earthly parents. Paul stresses the fact that we live in a non-separated state with Christ in us. Paul's epistles are so misunderstood because he knew and taught that he was never separated from the Christ in him.

Paul did not need an outer manifestation of God to convince him of God's presence because he understood that he was in a non-separated state with Christ. On television, you will be told God is real because you can see what He is doing. My reaction to such a statement is that Jesus of Nazareth performed much greater miracles than we see today, but those miracles changed very few hearts. Most of the people He ministered to did not show up when He needed a follower. Most of them did not believe to the end. Where were the dead who were raised when He was crucified? Where were the people He healed? Although these people received tremendous blessings, their lives were not changed. The Apostle Paul saw that it is Christ in us who meets our real needs.

The Outer Versus the Inner

We have the idea that for God to be God He has to do something outside of us to meet human needs. If you were dying with cancer and you were praying for God to come and heal you, I would most likely say the Healer is in you. I would want to turn your mind from the outer to the inner because once you begin to feast upon the fact that Christ lives in you, the outer doesn't matter anymore. Paul came to this understanding vividly when he said, *It doesn't matter whether I live or die* (Rom. 14:8). The outer did not determine who Paul was. Being poor or being rich did not determine who he was, for he said, *"I know both how to be abased, and I know how to abound"* (Phil. 4:11–12). What happened to him in his body did not matter. He was no longer becoming who he was for God by what happened on the outside of him. Paul was not a body person, as his body did not determine who he was anymore.

I can remember people through the years who put faith in their faith so that when God did not give them what they wanted, they almost quit God altogether. Years ago, I met a fellow who was a strong word-of-faith preacher who had vowed that God was going to heal him of his heart trouble. Finally, he was placed in a hospital attached to a respirator, and the doctor told him he was sorry but there was no more that could be done for him. The man broke down and wept and literally cursed God, after being a preacher and a lover of the Lord all his life. He had put faith in his faith, and it had failed him. People don't like to hear me say this because I tell them God may heal you every time you are sick, except the last time. God is going to take you home to His house one way or another. My body and my last thought belong to the Lord. Your needs will be met if you have the attitude that Christ in you is what you really need. The Apostle Paul's relationship with the Lord was one of such union that it did not matter what he was talking about because his thoughts and words, regardless of the subject, could be a prayer. This is an answer to the prayer that Jesus prayed in John 17.

In John 17:22–23, Jesus said, *"That they may be one, even as we are one: I in them, and thou in me, that they may be made perfect in one."* As you think about this relationship Jesus prayed for, do you believe Jesus received an answer to that prayer? He prayed that you would be one with Him and with the Father, a trinity, with the believer, the Father and the Son. If you are one with Him, then you are in a non-separated state with the Father and the Son; and you can expect that every word you say and every thought you have can be in oneness with the Father and the Son. That means every word can be a prayer. As Paul said, you can *"pray without ceasing"* (1 Thess. 5:17).

From my point of view, there are two kinds of prayer. Prayer that comes from the non-separated state you have with Christ in you and prayer that Jesus of Nazareth admonished us to have when we go into our closet and shut the door. They are both good, but the believer in Christ has the possibility of being constantly in a non-separated state from Christ. The only way you are in a non-separated state from Christ is in your thinking (this is the real faith). Therefore, if your mind is focused on the Lord who is in you, it doesn't matter what your conversation is; it will be a prayer. The world would then see a true Christian because your words would be out of a non-separated state with the Christ in you.

If you believed that when you get up in the morning it is Jesus as you, it is Jesus as you in your car, it is Jesus as you on the job, you would most likely watch what you say and do. The in-Christ message has changed us from outer thinking to inner thinking. As we are Christ-persons, we simply follow and are given to the Christ within.

Many think worship is jumping up and down, hollering, clapping their hands, and praising God, but that is more sensual than it is spiritual. Paul understood that all of our activities are worship. Therefore, he told us to do a good job, put in a good day's work, treat your fellowman right, treat your servants right, and for servants to treat their masters right. What he meant is that it is Christ as you doing it. It is His life coming through you. To really see the difference between the outer and the inner we need to look at 1 Corinthians 13.

The Problem with the Outer

The setting of 1 Corinthians 13 is the city of Corinth. Corinth was an idolatrous city whose goddess was Diana. The people of Corinth were involved in idolatrous worship, and the entire region worshipped the goddess Diana because she performed miracles. There were signs, wonders, and miracles associated with the goddess Diana. When people get caught up in this sort of thing—even demon worship—they are sure they are seeing signs, wonders, and miracles. Satan can do that sort of thing. When Paul came to the Christians in Corinth, they were still very much into the outer things. The outer things in this case had been idolatrous, and they believed in these idols for miracles. Many of these idolatrous, outer things were carried over into their lives as Christians because they felt that to know God is to have things happening in the outer.

In 1 Corinthians 12, the Apostle Paul put labels on these outer things by describing the nine gifts of the Spirit. In chapter 14, Paul corrected these outer things by telling the Corinthians how they are to operate within a group and as individuals. First Corinthians 13 is an important document because it is an intricate part of a bridge that the Scriptures build from self-ministry to Christ-ministry. Beginning at verse 1, Paul said,

> *Though I speak with the tongues of men and of angels, and have not charity, I am become as sounding brass, or a tinkling cymbal. And though I have the gift of prophecy, and understand all mysteries, and all knowledge; and though I have all faith, so that I could remove mountains, and have not charity, I am nothing.*

The first thing Paul does is to identify all the outer things that are taking place. Notice they were all outer, such as speaking in tongues of men and angels, revealing prophecy, understanding mysteries, having all knowledge, having all faith, and removing mountains. Not one of them had to do with a person's spirituality or relationship to the Father. The Christ-in-you relationship is with the Father who has birthed you. This relationship goes much deeper than what He can do through you or how He can use you. You are once and for all a birthed child of God, an offspring of God, by the implanting of the incorruptible seed in you (1 Peter 1:23). Christians are different; they are supposed to be different so the world will know the Christ who is in them.

The second thing Paul mentioned is that if I am able to do all these outer things, and I don't have love, I am nothing. I think when we read the entirety of Paul's writings, we see that the love affair Paul had was never with the things God could do. His love affair was with the Christ in him. It is important that you see the difference I am describing. I could tell you I love the works of God; however, that would focus on the outer things, which is not the gospel Paul brought to us. My love affair is not with buildings, doctrine, ministers, or ministries. My love affair is with the Christ within me. If I don't have this kind of love, I am nothing, which is the real heart of the matter. Paul said to these people who were prophesying and speaking in tongues that unless they had a love affair, they were nothing. He did not say the works were nothing or that those works were bad, but he limited them in chapter 14. He did say believers were nothing if these works became more important than Christ in them. That statement has gravity to it.

I once met a minister who had read my books, and he told me that if he preached this message everyone would forsake him. I told him the question should be whether or not it is truth. He admitted it was truth, but he said he could not preach it. He was not willing to love the Christ in him enough to preach it. That is a decision some people make. Paul's attitude was, *If Christ is my all, then my concept of ministry must change.* In Galatians 2:20 he said, in effect, *I am nothing because I am crucified with Christ.* Paul became nothing at the Cross because he was crucified with Christ. He became nothing, and Christ became his all. Seven times in Paul's epistles he said, *I am nothing* in one way or another. Have you ever agreed with the spirit of the world that says, *You have to believe that you are someone or something? You have to believe you are great, or important? If you don't love yourself, you have a problem?* That kind of thinking will fail you in the end. You can pump yourself up for a little while, but it will always be temporary. It will fail you because it is not your real life! It is like trying to be spiritual by resolving to pray as you have never prayed before, or to believe as you have never believed before. That is all within yourself, and you will fail at that attempt. It is good that you fail because you are nothing. Paul said to the Corinthians, *You are nothing. It does not matter how much you speak in tongues, how much you prophesy, or how many sick people you help. No matter how many people you reach with your message, you are nothing.* That is something you must understand in your mind. What really matters is your love affair with Christ.

In the next few verses of 1 Corinthians 13, Paul gave a parallel of what happens when you have a love affair going on with Christ. I want to skip down to verse 8: *"Charity never faileth: but whether there be prophecies, they shall fail; whether there be tongues, they shall cease; whether there be knowledge, it shall vanish away."* Paul described the temporary nature of our ministry. Tongues, prophecy, and manmade knowledge don't substitute for Christ. Prophecy, tongues, and any other thing we call supernatural ministries, are perfect from God until they hit our mind. Then they are no better than we are. For example, Isaiah and Amos both prophesied the same message from God in the same time period. Isaiah was a silver-tongued prophet and took 60 chapters to talk about it, while Amos took about 13 chapters because he was an unlearned farm boy. Paul was telling us that these outer things are not as important as your love affair with Christ. Paul said love never fails, but prophecies will fail, tongues will cease, and knowledge shall vanish away; they are all outer things. Paul did not say those things were wrong, but he did say they will pass away. If you had been in my meetings 30 years ago, you would have seen nothing but the outer things. Many people called me a prophet. I was always prophesying and speaking in tongues. When I found this love affair with Jesus those things slowly passed away.

A New Look at Prayer

Let me go a step further. I said to a group when the subject of prayer came up, "You know, I have almost quit asking God for things, I hardly ever ask God for anything for myself." One of the men who was a preacher spoke up and said, "You know that happened to me also and I have been afraid to mention it because I thought something was wrong with me." He continued by saying, "I have no desire to ask God for anything for myself anymore." So, it went around the table. What had happened to us was that our desires have been swallowed up by a love affair with Christ in us. I do pray, and if you tell me you have a need, I remember it and pray for you, but I seldom ask God for anything for myself.

Recently, it looked to me as if I was going to miss a meeting because of an air transportation problem. I have very seldom missed a meeting in many years of air travel through all kinds of weather. It struck me that my record was going to be ruined if something did not happen. I was tempted to say, God do this thing for me, but the Spirit checked me and said, "Do you think the circumstance you are in has changed the Father from loving you, taking care of you, and watching over you?" I decided not to ask Him to help me. That was a good thing because He had already worked it out and I did not know it. The outer looked to me as if I had to do something about it. Have you ever found that if you left things alone, He already had it in hand and it was taken care of, but you became nervous and aware that something outer needed to be done? What is happening to many believers is the love affair has changed from the outer to the inner. I don't need the outer things for God to be God and for me to be His son.

Paul declared in 1 Corinthians 13:9–10, *"For we know in part, and we prophesy in part. But when that which is perfect is come, then that which is in part shall be done away."* We don't talk about these verses much, do we? In my lifetime, I have had three different understandings of these Scriptures. In my Baptist days, we believed these things passed away when the Scriptures became completed. In my Pentecostal days, we preached "that which is perfect" would come on the resurrection morning and until then, we go on with the imperfect. Pentecostals and Charismatics will actually tell you we don't have the perfect but we have a part of it. However, Paul said, *"That which is in part shall be done away,"* and verse 11 says that is what is supposed to happen: *"When I was a child, I spake as a child, I understood as a child, I thought as a child: but when I became a man, I put away childish things."* Paul was finishing building the bridge by bringing us from the outer things to the inner things. The child ministry is explained in 1 John 2:12–14, where he gives us the three levels of understanding—child level, son level, and father level. The child level requires someone else must do it for you. In the church at Corinth, people prophesied, and those sitting around listened to them. Someone else spoke in tongues and another gave an interpretation. This is the child level. Paul said we should put aside the childish things. The son level is that it is not someone else doing it, rather we are doing it. Those at the son level know they have power over the Devil. The father level is when we know what God is doing from the beginning. "The beginning" is *"According as he has chosen us in him* [Christ] *before the foundation of the world"* (Eph. 1:4). In 1 Corinthians 13:11–12, Paul told us how we are going to see Christ. He said, *Until you put away childish things—which is someone else doing the ministry for you—you see through a glass darkly; but in time, when you put away childish things, you begin to see face to face. You need to see Christ, the one who is perfect.* The only thing about us that is perfect is Christ. The only thing about religion that is perfect is Christ. The only thing perfect about the Church is Christ. So he said, *"we see face to face."* That means our faces look into the face of Jesus, who is the Word. We look into the Scriptures as though they are a mirror. We see Jesus in the Scriptures, and He reflects back on us. We see Him face to face. When you start out, you are going to know in part, but in time you will know even as you are known, and that last line of verse 12 is the key: *"But then shall I know even as also I am known."* What you are to find out in the Christian life is who you are. God created you to be someone for His glory, and only with Christ in you can you ever become that. When you know Christ is in you, you will know who you are. Paul said by looking into the face of Jesus, you become who you were created to be.

Christ Being Expressed from Within

In Ephesians 3:17, Paul prayed, *"That Christ may dwell in your hearts by faith."* You must understand the terminology used here by Paul. He did not say he was praying that you have Christ in you. He was praying for you, that you will let Christ dwell in your hearts. You already have Christ's Spirit, and you are one with Him. But He has not come out through your mind yet. The heart is a part of the soul, which includes your mind, will, and emotions. Paul said you have Him in spirit, now let Him come out in your soul also. What you feel sensually outside of you is a belief in an outer Christ rather than Christ dwelling in you. If you go to a meeting, you may be lifted up. I always get stirred when someone triumphs over evil. If you have ever had those feelings, that was the outer. However, Paul said you don't come from outside inward for this anointing; you come from inside outward. Christ is in you, but He is not necessarily in your heart, which is soulish, because that is where the Holy Spirit works. The Holy Spirit's purpose is to reveal Christ to you in order to bring the knowledge of Christ from your spirit into your soul (heart). It is temporary and fleeting if you let it come from outside to inside, and it is not real. Paul's prayer, *"That Christ may dwell in your hearts by faith,"* describes a soulish action.

Eph. 3:18 continues, *"[That you] may be able."* The key word here is the word *able*. Paul used this word many times, but seven times he referred to the Christ in us who is able to do anything and everything. He is able; you are not able. *"[That you] may be able to comprehend with all saints what is the breadth, and length, and depth, and height; And to know the love of Christ"* (vv. 18–19). Two words used in these verses are absolutely necessary to your spiritual growth: the word *comprehend* in verse 18 and the word *know* in the first part of verse 19. These words are soulish words, having to do with knowledge and understanding in your mind and heart. You have Christ in you, but if you don't comprehend Him, it does not matter. If you don't know with all the saints the length, depth, and height of what is yours in Christ Jesus, you will never become who you were created to be. You have all the fullness of God in you, but you are not filled with it until you turn your soul and mind over to the Christ who is in you. How potent these verses are! But it is the following verse I really want you to see.

"Now unto him that is able" is the second of the seven times this word able is used in connection with the in-Christ message in Paul's writings. *"Now unto him that is able to do exceeding abundantly above all that we ask or think, according to the power that worketh in us"* (Eph. 3:20). I want to say two things about this verse. First, it tells us our doing and asking may get in the way of our receiving. In the kingdom message, Jesus of Nazareth said, *"Ask, and it shall be given you; seek, and ye shall find; knock, and it shall be opened unto you"* (Matt. 7:7). That is you doing something. You have to keep doing, and keep asking, and keep knocking. I have always loved the picture of Jesus knocking on a door, which is so common in our understanding. However, in the case of believers, He is not on the outside trying to get in. He is on the inside of believers trying to get out! We have it backwards. The kingdom message says if you keep working at things long enough then something good will happen to you. Actually, Paul said the opposite. *"Now unto Him that is able to do exceeding abundantly above all that we ask or think"* (Eph. 3:20). The more complete your understanding that Christ is your life, the less you are going to ask of Him. You don't ask because you live in the consciousness that it is Christ who is your life. The second thing to note is how God accomplishes this, *"according to the power that worketh in us."* That is where we started with Paul's revelation, Christ in you, your hope of glory (Col. 1:27). What is working in you at all times is Christ. If you are more interested in Him doing some-

thing outside of you than in Him working through you, you have missed the point of real Christianity. Christ is always working in us to do greater things, but you have to give Him a mind. Giving Him your mind is how you meet your need, and that is how you meet the needs of others.

Chapter 9
Review Questions

1. What does it mean to you that another person, Christ, lives in you?

2. Describe what you think the expression "outer things" means.

3. What does it mean to live in a non-separated state with Christ?

4. Explain what Romans 14:8 means to you.

5. Describe what you think the author means when he says it is important that we have "a love affair" with the Christ who is in us.

6. Explain what you think the words *fathers*, *young men*, and *little children* mean in 1 John 2:13–14.

7. How can you best help another to have their needs met?

Then Agrippa said unto Paul, Thou art permitted to speak for thyself. Then Paul stretched forth the hand, and answered for himself ... King Agrippa, believest thou the prophets? I know that thou believest. Then Agrippa said unto Paul, Almost thou persuadest me to be a Christian. And Paul said, I would to God, that not only thou, but also all that hear me this day, were both almost, and altogether such as I am, except these bonds ... Then said Agrippa unto Festus, This man might have been set at liberty, if he had not appealed unto Caesar. (Acts 26:1, 27–29, 32)

CHAPTER 10
Paul and the Birthing

Introduction

In order to understand the birthing or what it means to be born again, a little history might be helpful. In the Old Testament, salvation was of the soul. That sounds very simple because as we grew up in religion we have had soul-winning campaigns and everyone was encouraged to be a soul winner. The use of the word *soul* is really Old Testament terminology. In the Old Testament, the saving of a soul was all there could be. There was no saving of the spirit by Christ coming into the believer's spirit because Christ was not yet in that form. Christ had not died on the cross, and Paul had not had his revelation of the mystery. It was not possible to have a change in spirit wrought by Christ in the believer at the time of the Old Testament. All soul salvation is of self, meaning you must do something to make it happen. Abraham was a great man of faith, but the Scriptures state that what made him a great man was obedience, which is self-effort. Obedience-salvation requires that you do something to make it work. All salvation in the entire Old Testament was soulish. There was no change in spirit, meaning Christ was not joined to a person's spirit.

In the Old Testament, the word *soul* is used 10 times more than in the New Testament. In Paul's epistles, he uses the word *soul* less than 10 times all together. There is so little mention of soul in the New Testament because once Christ was joined to the spirit of the believer, there was not anything you could do to improve the condition of your spirit. In the Old Testament, salvation was something you did soulishly, and you brought your spirit (Adamic nature) under subjection. That was very tenuous because even the greatest people in the Old Testament had a difficult time bringing their spirit under subjection.

Salvation by Grace

When Paul received his revelation of the mystery, he understood that God did something. Man had nothing to do with this revelation at all. In a way, salvation was reversed. You may recall the three tenses of salvation discussed in chapter 6 on "Paul and The Mind." Spirit salvation is finished and is perfect. Soul is in the process of being saved. Body is not saved and will not be saved until the resurrection morning when the corruptible puts on incorruption. Keeping this in mind, we are able to see something very distinct about salvation. Salvation of the soul works from Christ coming from our spirit into our soul. This is a difficult thing for believers to understand. Far too many believers keep working the outer things—such as church duties, doctrines, beliefs, creeds, good works, and other self-efforts—into their soul/mind, believing this will make them better Christians. This is all to no avail, especially to the Christ in us. It is His life within working to the outer man that makes a bona fide Christian.

Hebrews 4:12 says, *"For the word of God is quick, and powerful, and sharper than any twoedged sword, piercing even to the dividing asunder of soul and spirit."* Paul made a distinction between soul and spirit. In effect, he said you should no longer understand that the Spirit of the Lord, or any special anointing coming upon you, forms a spiritual relationship. For instance, by dividing soul and spirit, you will know that you can never do anything within yourself to bring about the birthing. You must separate soul from spirit if you are to mature in the Lord. Separating soul and spirit makes your calling and your election sure. Knowing the division of soul and spirit allows you to know you are right with God, every moment of every day to your dying breath. That knowledge eliminates retaliation, which is why most of us sin. Without that knowledge of our right standing before God, we are frustrated because we are not putting life together. Therefore, we retaliate by doing something that hurts us, hurts God, or hurts someone else. Nine out of 10 church constitutions are soulish because they tell you what you must do to be one of them or to be a good Christian. Until we know the separation between soul and spirit, we will never understand our salvation; and unless we have that understanding, we will never walk in truth.

I am not saying you will be sinless in the flesh. What you will experience is that your life will be considerably different, and you will know that the grace of God alone is sufficient for your salvation. The Word of God tells us that this is so. Most of us read one verse of Scripture that is conditional and conclude that if we don't do a certain thing we are going to lose out with God or even go to hell. Then we pick up another verse of Scripture that tells us we are saved to the uttermost. Because our minds are not renewed, we believe the negative more than we believe the positive. That is because the nature that has had the greatest influence over our life was Satan's sin-nature. Satan's nature indwelt our spirit for a time, and it ruled us until we became born again. Our minds now need to be renewed because of his abuse.

Rightly Dividing
The ability to rightly divide the Word of Truth is what gives understanding of salvation. Paul said of Peter in Galatians 2:11, *"I withstood him to the face."* Paul told Peter to go and preach circumcision (law) to the Jews (Gal. 2:7), and Paul was determined to take the gospel of uncircumcision (grace) to the Gentiles.

That is where this message starts. Most Christians are so accustomed to commingling the two gospels that they fail to see the necessity of rightly dividing the Scriptures. The great error in not rightly dividing the Scriptures is it builds various erroneous ideas and doctrines of what salvation really is. Salvation is Christ in you (Col. 1:27). Salvation is being baptized (placed) into Christ (1 Cor. 12:13). Salvation is the cessation of the old life (Gal. 2:20). Salvation is becoming a new creature (2 Cor. 5:17). Salvation is being crucified, buried, resurrected, and ascended with Christ. Finally, salvation is a Father placing His incorruptible seed, Christ, in the believing sinner (1 Peter 1:23). This definition of what salvation is could go on endlessly; but to know the truth of what salvation is, one has to study Paul's epistles. The proof not found anywhere else in the Bible is there.

When rightly dividing the Scriptures, it is just as important to know what salvation is not. Salvation is not the betterment of the human being; it is the believer coming to a whole other life, the Christ-life. Salvation is not church membership, and it has nothing to do with church buildings, ministers, religious programs, or doctrines.

Salvation has no connection to good works. Good works come out of it, but they don't make it valid. Salvation is not based on what the human does to be saved, but relies solely on what the Father has done at Calvary. Salvation has no biblical connection with water baptism in grace or in Paul's epistles. Salvation is the work of God at the Cross. Water baptism is the work of man; it is religion and human effort to report something that has already taken place. Salvation is not of the law, nor does it have anything to do with Moses' Law, the Torah, the Ten Commandments, or self-effort. This contrast between what salvation is and what it is not could be as large as the Bible. Because of this, Paul said we must rightly divide the Scriptures to exactly know what to believe as well as to know what the Father has done to save people from sin.

One time a young man came to me who was really upset. He said he based his relationship with the Lord on Ezekiel 36:25. That particular verse is one of the covenants that belong to Israel. *"Then will I sprinkle clean water upon you, and ye shall be clean: from all your filthiness, and from all your idols, will I cleanse you."* Certain holiness people have taken that verse so literally that they even wash feet and re-baptize you in water to make sure you are cleansed. But notice this section of Scripture belongs to Israel (see verse 32). We are too quick to take Scriptures for ourselves that don't belong to us. Verse 26 goes on to say, *"A new heart also will I give you, and a new spirit will I put within you: and I will take away the stony heart out of your flesh, and I will give you an heart of flesh."* Such Scriptures make it imperative that we rightly divide. This Scripture belongs solely to Israel. It is totally an outer work of God to make Israel acceptable to God. There is no birthing. We know this all belongs to Israel, for verse 28 of this same passage says, *"And ye shall dwell in the land that I gave to your fathers."* That separates us right there. The born-again have no land. We belong in the Father's house. We own nothing on this earth. He chose us to live in His house from the very beginning. You must rightly divide the Word of Truth to understand what the birthing is all about.

These verses are all soulish! Anytime God is dealing with our heart, it is soulish. Certainly, when we hear the gospel, our heart is touched; but that is not where salvation is. Salvation does not consist of our being touched by God. Your spiritual birthing (being born again) is not in something you do, just as your physical birth had nothing to do with something you did. The birthing is something God does. It is an exchanged life—Satan's nature out, Christ and the God-nature in.

Another thing is important at this point. Isaiah 55:6 reads, *"Seek ye the Lord while he may be found, call ye upon him while he is near."* This verse has no relationship to spiritual rebirth. It is speaking of something we must do, seek. Jesus said in Luke 19:10, *"For the Son of man is come to seek and to save that which was lost."* There is a huge difference between my seeking God and trying to get hold of Him, and Christ seeking me! I should not have any confidence that I am going to find the Lord on my own.

What makes most of you read this book? Because there are not many places you can go to find this message. Actually, you are not supposed to go somewhere to find this message. The reason you don't seek after the Lord is because He is not far from you. He is in you! In one gospel, you are always seeking after the Lord; and in the other gospel, He is seeking after you. The world today is disillusioned with religion and Christianity because we don't realize that this Christ in us is trying to get hold of our minds. People who have believed on the Lord Jesus Christ have Christ in them because that is the only kind of salvation God offers in this time period we are in, the Dispensation of Grace. Christ in you is seeking to control your mind. He wants control of your life.

Entering into the Things of God

When Jesus spoke to Nicodemus one night, He said two things. First, He said, *"Except a man be born again, he cannot see the kingdom of God"* (John 3:3). I don't think we have ever placed the weight on being born again that Jesus did. When have you ever heard anyone put the kind of stress on being born again that emphasizes seeing the kingdom of God? We are told to be born again so we won't go to hell. Others are told if they are born again, their problems will be over and they will be like the rest of us. Do you know anyone who said being born again is the key to unlocking the door to see and enter into the things of God? It isn't just a question of avoiding hell and getting to heaven, or a question of being saved. It is a question of entering into the things of God, of entering into the fullness of Christ.

If you were to ask me what is wrong with religion today, I would say religious people don't enter into the things of God. Their interest and emphasis is on "how-to" religion—how to save your marriage, how to save your children, how to get along with others, how to make money, how to save money. These interests are all soulish interests. Consequently, Jesus is right there joined to their spirit and wondering when He can get out of His locked room. Will He have to wait until the resurrection morning? Most likely, that is going to happen with many Christians.

I have a paraphrase for John 3:16 to explain that the Father came to the ultimate act of love, which is cohabitation. My paraphrase is, *For the Father so loved the sinner that He cohabited with the sinner and gave the sinner His only Son so he/she would not perish but have everlasting life.* That is my introduction to the birthing, which is God's act of love—cohabiting with the sinner and placing His seed (His Son with His nature) in the sinner to be the life of that sinner. That is the ultimate of God's love. John never let go of this idea of the birthing and carried it throughout his writings.

Let us look at another statement written by John in 1 John 3:9, *"Whosoever is born* [birthed] *of God ..."* I take the liberty of using *birthed* for the word *born*. In this verse, the word *born* or *birthed* is used twice. Notice why I have done this. The verse says, *"Whosoever is* [birthed] *of God doth not commit sin."* It does not say could not commit sin or would not commit sin. It says, he *"does not commit sin."* How are you going to handle that verse? If you don't understand the birthing, there is no way you can understand that statement. Newer translations of the Bible say something like *whosoever is born of God does not practice sinning.* Does that sound the same to you? I believe the verse means just what it says. When the believer was birthed in Christ, he became one with Christ so that the only life he now has to live is Christ. He could live in another manner, but it would not be life. I would call it death-life. If Christ is in the believer, it means Christ's life is not a sinning life and cannot sin. I am not saying the believer cannot sin soulishly because John said in 1 John 1:8, *"If we say that we have no sin, we deceive ourselves, and the truth is not in us."* In chapter 3, John is not talking about a sinless believer but a sinless life. You have to understand who is your life. To God, the real me is not the whole man because my body is not yet saved and my soul is in the process of being saved. When God looks at me, He sees Christ in me. *"But of him are ye in Christ Jesus, who of God is made unto us wisdom, and righteousness, and sanctification, and redemption"* (1 Cor. 1:30). That is what God sees when he looks at me. How do I know Christ in me is the real me? In Paul's own words, *"Christ, who is our life"* (Col. 3:4) and *"Christ liveth in me"* (Gal. 2:20). Paul says my life is not soulish; my life is in the Son! John reinforces this by saying, *"He that hath the Son hath life; and he that hath not the Son of God hath not life"* (1 John 5:12). The only place you have life is in the Son, who lives in the believer. Christ was birthed, or born, in you. Without an understanding of the birthing, you will never understand Christianity.

There are three parts that comprise the birthing. There must be a father, there must be a seed, and there must be a vessel in which that seed produces another person. God's plan of how another lives in us is explained in the Epistle of 1 John. *"Beloved, let us love one another: for love is of God"* (1 John 4:7). It is obvious that John is talking about something other than what we feel, know, and understand about love. Love is of God because God so loved. The Cross is the first time we can understand God's love because love is expressed by Jesus dying on the cross. Love is a God-thing; and until we understand this concept, life is going to be difficult for us.

What Is Love?

Everyone is trying to figure out love today. Hollywood, television, and other segments of our culture have actually minimized what true love really means. A high percentage of marriages today end in divorce, with the attitude that they loved each other for a while, but they don't love each other anymore. God's plan and God's Word are made mockeries because we don't understand love. First John 4:8 says, *"For God is love."* God does not give love; He is love. Love is of God, and without God, you don't have true love.

"Beloved, let us love one another: for love is of God; and every one that loveth is born [birthed] *of God, and knoweth God"* (1 John 4:7). Two things in this verse are important to the birthing. The first is that we must learn to love in a different manner. We were all raised in an environment to love "if" or "because." Love should be greatest in a church building, but the world knows this is not so. Many people in church buildings think they have rights to do everything they do, but the world takes one look and says that is not love.

An important concept we believers must understand is the basis by which we judge another. Our only basis for judging another should be whether or not Jesus is in them. However, if Christ is not in them, then we must take their hand, in love, and lead them to

Christ. I also know it is not in me to love. I have tried to love people by earnestly praying for God to help me to love people. I did everything I could for people who were unloving to one another. I have prayed for hundreds of marriages, trying to get them to love one another. But true love is seeing Jesus in each other, and whoever is birthed of God sees Christ. I either see Christ in you or I see through you to Christ.

The second thing 1 John 4:7 says is those who are birthed of God *"knoweth God."* That is a very important verse connected with the birthing. Sometimes people get upset with me and say all I talk about is the Father. They want me to talk more about the Son, but the Son in me is one with the Father. In John 17:20–21, Jesus prayed that we would be one with Him as He is with the Father. The most important thing we can ever know about God is that He is a Father. He is not only Almighty God. He is not only a sovereign God. He is not only the Creator God. He is my Father! That is what Jesus came to tell the Jews. They killed Him because He said God was His Father. The Jews wanted to be children of Abraham. It is ironic that there is only one verse I have found in the entire Bible calling Israel "children of God." They never were His children. They were always children of Israel and could not be children of God because He did not birth them. The nation of Israel still has not been rebirthed and will not be rebirthed until she returns to God as a nation and accepts her Messiah. When a Jew is born again in this present Dispensation of Grace, he is no longer a Jew to God. He is a new creation like all the rest of us, and there is no difference between Jew and Gentile for those who are in the Body of Christ (Rom. 10:12; Gal. 3:28; Col. 3:11).

Sometimes the load gets so heavy, the persecution so great, the times in your life so difficult, that you need a Heavenly Father. The heavens will seem like brass, and you will not have an ounce of your own faith to try to get an answer. Eventually, this will drive you to the understanding that God is your Father, and it is Christ in you who is the answer.

Learning the Christ in us is the big issue of life. Jesus said, *"He that hath seen me hath seen the Father"* (John 14:9). We still have not seen Jesus clearly, yet the Jesus that we do not know is in us. Believers know all about Jesus in the Old Testament, Jesus of Nazareth, Jesus in the Tribulation period, and Jesus in the Millennium, but they don't know the Jesus who is in them. We can only know our Father by learning Christ.

The Birthing

In 1 John 5:1 we read, *"Whosoever believeth that Jesus is the Christ is born* [birthed] *of God: and every one that loveth Him that begat* [birthed] *loveth Him also that is begotten* [is birthed] *of him."* What we have in this verse are three different terms relating to the birthing—*born, begat,* and *begotten.* All three words mean the same thing, and they have to do with the birthing (being birthed of God). You cannot get away from the birthing in John's epistles and John's gospel. The birthing stands out powerfully and significantly in both writings.

Skipping down to 1 John 5:4 we read, *"For whatsoever is born* [birthed] *of God overcometh the world: and this is the victory that overcometh the world, even our faith."* Now this verse takes some explaining. It states whosoever is born of God overcometh the world. It is very rare to hear anyone preach on that statement. What you usually hear is that the born-again have ready access to God or the born-again can get faith to obtain a miracle. This verse does not say there is anything you have to do to make it work. Instead, it says the birthing means you have overcome the world. That is hard on us because we don't really believe this fact.

Moreover, we are too mixed up with all the soulish preaching telling us to seek after God, to fast and pray, to memorize the Scriptures, and to get hold of someone who has the faith that can help us. At the same time, this verse does not say whoever is birthed of God will never have trouble. This verse does not say you will not get sick. It does not say you will never die.

The moment we were born again, we became unfit for this world. We are not supposed to fit in because we are a new creation. We are an entirely different race of people, like people from Venus or Mars who have set foot on this earth. God Himself rebirths us, and He did not intend that the world should swallow us up. The world and all that is in it is under His subjection. *"All things were created by him and for him,"* and aside from Christ there is nothing in existence (Col. 1:16–17). Furthermore, John said, *"All things were made by him; and without him was not anything made that was made"* (John 1:3). While the world was created with its evil, its tree of knowledge, with the serpent, and it grew full of evil men all around, and it continues to get worse and worse, God still says whoever is birthed of God overcomes the world. We have not heard this gospel have we? What a difference it would make if every Christian knew Christ was in them and that learning Christ would mean it did not matter what the Devil threw at them. They would be overcomers, regardless of what God allowed to come their way or what they had to go through. If there is a layoff on the job, it concerns us. If the necessary money does not come in, it concerns us. If the doctor says there is a lump, that concerns us. From now until the time we go home to the Father's house, there are going to be things that concern us. God has overcome the world. Nevertheless, the Scriptures don't say it will not hurt or it will not get bad. They do say we will overcome.

I don't know what you are concerned about, but I want to tell you that your visible problem is not the real problem. Your problem is in knowing who you are because whoever is birthed by God is going to overcome this world. Better yet, you have already overcome because there is not anything in the world that can take away your birthing or your relationship with the Father. Paul saw this, and he thought of one of the worst things that could happen to a human being, and that was dying. Then he said it does not matter whether I live or die. I have often told people on their deathbed that Christ was in them. Hearing that made a big change in them because they were frightened to meet God, and most of them were wondering why God did not give them a miracle and raise them out of bed. They had forgotten—or they did not know—that Christ was in them.

First John 5:18 says, *"We know that whosoever is born* [birthed] *of God sinneth not; but he that is begotten* [birthed] *of God keepeth himself, and that wicked one toucheth him not."* Some Charismatics and Pentecostals would rather chase the Devil than preach a gospel that says the Devil does not touch whoever is birthed of God.

A remarkable thing happened to me years ago. It may have been my Baptist background, since we were never taught much about the Devil. When I began to preach in Pentecostal and Charismatic churches, all I heard about was the Devil. Gradually, I became Devil-conscious. Later, I decided that if I were the Devil I would want people to be conscious of me. If I were the Devil, I would want everyone casting out devils and calling everything from a stubbed toe to a burned-down house the work of the Devil. By distracting them with Devil-consciousness, there would be fewer opportunities for them to know that whoever is birthed of God cannot be touched by the Devil without God's permission. That is a big thing, isn't it?

This verse also says, *"He that is begotten of God keepeth himself."* We need to ask ourselves how that works. A believer cannot save himself, and he cannot stay saved on his own. How then does he keep himself? I think the answer is by doing what he knows he ought to do to be true to the Christ within him. Again, this is the best thing James ever said, *"Therefore to him that knoweth to do good, and doeth it not, to him it is sin"* (James 4:17). Sin, then, is a violation of your knowledge. Think about a diabetic person. If a diabetic takes his pill or his insulin shot on schedule he lives. He is keeping himself by doing what he ought to do. Most of us don't do what we are supposed to do most of the time. You cannot have a love affair with Jesus until you know He is in you. Until you have this revelation, you are soulish when you want to be, and yet at other times you think you are spiritual. In truth, He is the perfect Spirit within you, and He is working out through you through your soul/mind.

Conclusion

I have spent time in this chapter underscoring what John said because he defines the word *birthing* for us. The most ironic thing in the Scriptures is that the Apostle Paul never used the expression *born again*, let alone the word *birthing*. It was John who paralleled our new birth with natural birth. God so loved that He committed an act of cohabitation with the sinner. When the Apostle Paul had his revelation of Christ in him, he saw something that not even John saw. He saw something that Jesus of Nazareth never fully commented on. When it was revealed to him that Christ was in him, the Apostle Paul saw it as a great mystery. It truly is a great mystery.

The religious world has thrown the term *born again* around without proper explanation. Paul said it is a mystery that goes far beyond human comprehension; therefore, it would have to be revealed to you.

Eye hath not seen, nor ear heard, neither have entered into the heart of man, the things which God hath prepared for them that love him. But God hath revealed them unto us by his Spirit.
(1 Cor. 2:9–10)

I study every book I think will take me in a direction of truth, yet I have never found anyone who writes about the revelation of the mystery. You need a revelation; otherwise, it is all head knowledge, and that keeps men soulish. At least 13 times, Paul speaks of the mystery *"which is Christ in you, the hope of glory"* (Col. 1:26–27). The great mystery is not just that you are born again; it is your only hope! The only hope you have is not Christ, but Christ in you. We know the Christ who gives us hope, but that is not the Jesus that Paul said we needed to know. The Jesus you need to know is the one who is in you. I take this message to heart. It is my desire to bring this message to you, but somewhere along the way the Spirit must reveal it to you.

In this chapter, I have brought out in John's writings what the birthing means, but that is not worth a nickel to you until you have a revelation of it. A preacher can say we are born again, but that is not the gospel. The gospel is not something that happened to us as an experience. The gospel is Christ in us. Paul said 146 times we are in Christ. The final understanding of this must come through the Holy Spirit. The Holy Spirit works in each soul to bring us to see Christ in us. That is why, when you are filled with the Holy Spirit, the power you receive is in this knowing. Jesus said He, the Spirit of truth, would not speak of himself but would testify of Christ when He comes (John 15:26; 16:13). That is what Christianity is all about.

Chapter 10
Review Questions

1. Describe how people in the Old Testament were saved.

2. Name and describe the three tenses of post-Calvary salvation.

3. Explain why it is important to be able to divide the soul from the spirit in your thinking.

4. In 1 John 5:18, the Scripture says he who is born of God *"keepeth himself."* How do you think a Christian keeps himself?

5. In what ways does being born again parallel our natural birthing?

And when it was determined that we should sail into Italy, they delivered Paul and certain other prisoners unto one named Julius, a centurion ... And entering into a ship ... we launched, meaning to sail by the coasts of Asia ... And when the ship was caught, and could not bear up into the wind, we let her drive ... [Paul said,] I exhort you to be of good cheer: for there shall be no loss of any man's life among you, but of the ship. For there stood by me this night the angel of God, whose I am, and whom I serve, Saying, Fear not, Paul; thou must be brought before Caesar: and, lo, God hath given thee all them that sail with thee ... that they which could swim should cast themselves first into the sea, and get to land: and the rest, some on boards, and some on broken pieces of the ship ... they escaped all safe to land. (Acts 27:1–2, 22–24, 43–44)

CHAPTER 11
Paul and Spiritual Growth

Introduction

It has not been easy for us to incorporate into our thinking the truth that Christ is our life, let alone the idea that He is our only life. However, in our reading of the Scriptures, we can see clearly that the Apostle Paul made a drastic change in his understanding of faith, the law, the Church, and the way he dealt with problems after he had Christ revealed in him. These changes were all in his thinking. In other words, Paul had to make some choices, and making choices is one of the most difficult things a human being can do. All life in the natural is made up of the choices you make. When people have something that fits into their lives, they don't want to change it, even if the idea they presently hold is wrong. If it fits into their lifestyle, they begin to believe that particular understanding is a part of who they are. Most people who begin drinking don't like their first drink; but after a while it begins to taste all right, and it becomes an addiction. They say to themselves, *This is who I am.* When you go to an Alcoholics Anonymous meeting, even those who have been dry for years get up and say, "I am an alcoholic." Even if they stop drinking, they don't want to make a change about who they are and the way they think.

The Process of Changing a Belief

When people hear the true gospel, they often don't want to change their thinking. Israel was delivered from Egyptian bondage, and several hundred years later she wanted to go back to Egypt. Israel could not make the change. Ethnic power in a family works the same way. You might be raised in an Italian family that lives thousands of miles from Italy, but because you are told enough stories about being an Italian, it forms in your mind and becomes your identity. It is the same with Christians. Christians are told something enough times until they are brainwashed, and they don't want to make any changes. Sometimes people come to our meetings and remark how the Lord showed them years ago something I had said during the meeting—but then I never see them again. The reason they don't return is they cannot make the change. They are married to their beliefs and cannot give up what has made them who they think they are.

When the Apostle Paul received a revelation of Christ in him, it was an awesome thing. The revelation confronted Paul with a choice. For example, when God said another person lived in Paul, Paul had to consider everything he was. It meant that if he took up this new life, the Christ-life, he had to do away with everything he was. He was a rabbi, and now nothing in his rabbinical background would be worthwhile if Christ was in him. He was a lawyer, and now nothing that made him a lawyer would stand or help him with this new information. He came from a rich family, a Hebrew family, and none of that mattered anymore. The message gripped him so firmly that he said there were no Jews in Christ Jesus. He was of the tribe of Benjamin, a special group, but that did not matter anymore. He said in Philippians 3:8 that he had suffered the loss of everything that made him what he was for the excellency of the knowledge of Christ Jesus his Lord. What a choice he made!

As Christians, we bring what we have to the Lord and said, "Lord, use it." We hear famous singers on television, and think that if they would give their hearts to the Lord, they could lead so many people to God. Our consciousness is that God needs their talent, or their personality, or their charisma. However, none of these things is a consideration to God. The person who comes to the Lord may have to suffer the loss of all of those things for this new knowledge. Going on with Christ has a lot more attached to it. Many people sit in churches for years and don't grow. The fact is that some churches themselves can prevent you from growing even if you want to grow. Everyone has had a move of the Spirit at one time or another, the Lord calling each one, but to make the choice is very difficult.

When the Apostle Paul made his choice, it was revolutionary. Many Christians serve the Lord and are happy for a little while, but then they start fussing and quit their churches or go into sin. Churches split apart because members are mad at each other, and they may even go to court against each other. Christian husbands and wives separate. I think the answer is that we don't understand what happened to us when we were saved. We don't know Christ was put in us and Christ in us does not need anything we were previously.

You, however, were the product of everything except the knowledge that Christ came into you to fulfill God's original intention of creating you in His likeness and image. This is the Father's only interest—to have Christ as your only life, which brings glory to God. It does not mean that all you have learned—your talents, your gifts, and your abilities—will not surface. They probably will, but as His rather than yours. That is a big difference! A person who is birthed and gifted to be a pianist or a musician may have to set those talents aside while Christ becomes his or her life. In time, those talents may again surface and will be Christ's gifts, Christ's ministries, and Christ's abilities. In order to grow spiritually, Paul suffered the loss of all these things for the excellency of the knowledge of Christ. If Christ lives in me, what can I add to His stature? What can I give that would add to His grace? I need to let Him be my all. As I grow into Him, becoming one with Him through learning Him (soul/mind), He can use whatever talents He wants. All will be His, but first He has to be my life. You don't start by turning all your gifts over to Him, but by renewing your mind that His life operates as you. In the past, He may have led you in a certain way, but now you will know they are not your gifts when they resurface. It is no longer your education, talent, or ability.

The Importance of Choices in Spiritual Growth

Spiritual growth is determined by your choices and not by how much you pray, how much you sing, or how spiritual you act. Spiritual growth is not determined by the outer things you do. Spiritual growth is not determined by whether you speak in tongues or whether you prophesy, which Paul called childish things (1 Cor. 13:8–11). Spiritual growth is when you resolve that He is your all and He is your only life.

To come to this place, you must have the Lord dealing in your life. I talk about circumstances and situations (the C & S gang) because they determine whether you will give up or whether you are going on in the Lord. A choice you must make in each situation is whether you will turn it over to the Father or carry the load yourself. Unfortunately, most of us carry the load and get nervous or upset with all the things that happen to us. We remain on this earth to renew our minds so that we may grow up into Him, to come to the full knowledge of Christ. We are not to be the head of the Body of Christ, but we can come to the knowledge of the Head. Living the Christ-life and becoming what God created you to be is where you make many choices. Speaking the truth in love is a challenge to us in the Christ-life because the world needs to see, hear, and act on this gospel.

By speaking the truth in love, we grow up into Him in all things, which include circumstances and situations. We need to see through circumstances and situations to Christ because that is how spiritual growth takes place. We see through everything because it all has to do with Christ. If you are having a problem on your job, it has to do with Christ. If you have problems at home, it has to do with Christ. If you have problems with the credit card company, it has to do with Christ. Everything has to do with Jesus Christ.

In Galatians 4:19 Paul writes, *"My little children, of whom I travail in birth again until Christ be formed in you."* When Paul preached this message, it was as if he were travailing as a woman about to bring forth a child. He said, I have birthed you through the gospel I preach (1 Cor. 4:15). That means he knew this gospel was so powerful that whenever he gave it out, he felt like he was in birth pains delivering life to the hearer.

There are two ways Galatians 4:19 can be taken. To put it bluntly, there is a religious way and a spiritual way. Most believers take the religious way and say, "God is not finished with me yet," as if God still has work to do because Christ is not fully formed in them. Notice the emphasis is not on the believer but on Christ. The believer does not have a changed life—a cleaned-up version of the same life—by the birthing. He has a new, completely different life (2 Cor. 5:17). Christianity is an exchanged life. We grow up in religion believing we don't have all and we need to seek God to get more. We need to go to a church to get more of God. If we don't read our Bible, we don't grow. If we don't give our money, we don't grow. We should not focus so much on what we are becoming but on Christ living in us. Many Christians don't know that Jesus is complete in them. Religion will try to keep you in a place where you think you don't have all of God. Thinking you need to do something to get all of God is "doer" religion.

Most of the commentaries on Galatians 4:19 suggest that Christ is not complete in you until you become faithful and pray more. However, that is not what the verse means. If that were so, there would be no such thing as an incorruptible seed. In 1 Peter 1:23, Peter said, *"Being born again, not of corruptible seed, but of incorruptible."* The word *incorruptible* not only means it is a pure and holy seed God put in you. It also means God's seed is a perfect seed. The Apostle Paul never presents Christ to the believer except as being total and complete. Colossians 2:10 declares, *"Ye are complete in him."* This means you cannot get just a little bit of Christ. When you were saved, you did not get just a part of Christ. The Scriptures teach that Christ's salvation is a finished work. The instant you believe, you stand in that finished work, with nothing for you to do. To say that Christ is not formed fully is contrary to the Word of God because Jesus is total.

In order to understand this truth, I would draw a circle around the word *you* in *"I travail in birth again until Christ be formed in you"* (Gal. 4:19). Christ is not being formed, as He is already complete and total. Paul meant you must allow Christ to be in every area of your life. The verse that best explains this is Ephesians 4:15, *"But speaking the truth in love, [you] may grow up into him in all things, which is the head, even Christ."* We are not growing up by our own effort; we are growing up into Him because He is complete and is all. From the time Paul made his choice that Jesus was not just his life but his all in all, he was convinced of this. Spiritual growth is allowing Jesus to be all things. The world does not know the real Jesus because they can only know Him by us. If we have not allowed Him to be in all things, it is difficult for them to see Him. When I speak with someone, I don't have to wear a sign that tells that person I am different. It should show and come forth in all the things I do.

Spiritual growth is not how much you prophesy, how much you speak in tongues, or how faithful you are to programs. Spiritual growth is allowing Him to manifest Himself in all things through you. The only Jesus on this earth is the Christ in the believer. Another Christian should never criticize that you are not righteous enough or not doing enough. That is foolishness. You could do all of those things and still have no spiritual growth. Nothing in life is accomplished if you don't grow up into Him. I often thought being able to speak in tongues and prophesy is why the Christ-life and grace message is so difficult for some people to accept. People are afraid of losing their identity and becoming something or someone contrary to what they previously believed they were. Spiritual growth is the release of what you have learned and who you think you are for new truth revealed by the Holy Spirit.

The Apostle Paul did not come to know Christ in him from studying Abraham or following Moses because they did not have Christ in them. There is no life in Abraham, and there is no life in Moses. The only way Paul could come to knowledge was by revelation. When Paul received a revelation of Christ in him, he did not mention one Old Testament character as having to do with Christianity. He did not even mention Jesus of Nazareth and His works—except His death, burial, and resurrection. He did not know Christ in the flesh. Spiritual growth starts at point zero: Christ in me is my hope of glory. Paul's spiritual growth was based on Christ, who was his only life and the only pleasing one to God. That is a different way to live. That is a different gospel. No wonder Paul called it "my gospel." No wonder Paul said, *"If any man preach any other gospel unto you than that ye have received, let him be accursed"* (Gal. 1:9).

When we were birthed, the Father's intention was that the Holy Spirit would teach us by revelation. Since I have had a revelation of Christ in me, all my knowledge and ideas have been vanquished by Him. Christ in me is my hope, and learning about Him supersedes questions about where Cain's wife came from or whether a whale really swallowed Jonah. It does not matter to me anymore. Nothing in the Old Testament matters. I worry about people who spend time trying to prove that God created the earth. The answer seems so simple to me. I just take what God says in His Word. If He does not tell me where Cain's wife came from, that is up to Him. I don't expect my Father to tell me everything.

Thus, revelation knowledge has overwhelmed all these concerns. Once God has revealed to me His Son in me, nothing else matters very much. Throughout my lifetime, I have read countless books from writers who try to explain the book of Revelation, and I wondered why they spent all that time earnestly trying to figure it all out. A greater fact is that hardly any two of them agreed. If God does not explain a truth or idea, then whatever man does is human speculation. I have not worried about the book of Revelation since I had Christ revealed in me. I expect to be raptured off this earth before any of the events mentioned in the book of Revelation. In the meantime, I focus on revelation knowledge above whatever happens in this world. I have a different kind of knowledge that enables me to face whatever issues come up in this world. Paul was able to say that in the issues of life and death, it does not matter anymore whether he lived or died. Of course, he took care of himself, but it did not matter in his mind because he was overwhelmed by revelation knowledge. Whether I am here or there, Paul said, it is still Christ.

Therefore, Spirit-taught revelation knowledge is a key by which you grow spiritually. You will always have bits and pieces of revelation knowledge during your earthly journey, but at some juncture you will get a clear revelation that the life in you is Christ. In 1 Corinthians 2:9–10, Paul very explicitly said the deeper things of God cannot be seen with the eyes, heard with the ear, or felt in the heart. Most Christians say they believe because God showed them. Paul would say that does not matter. Other Christians say, *Well, I heard the Spirit speak to me and that settled it for me.* Paul would say that does not matter. Still other Christians say, *I was in a great meeting, and I felt the presence and power of God and have never doubted Him since.* Paul would say that does not matter. I know my statements are very difficult for some because that is where we are as Christians. That is what made us Christians. A good question each of us should ask is, *If everything in my life that I have seen, heard, and felt was to be taken away from me, what would I believe?*

Revelation Knowledge

Revelation knowledge has nothing to do with what you see, hear, or feel. For Paul, it was what you know. Revelation knowledge is a knowing. *"Eye hath not seen, nor ear heard, neither have entered into the heart of man, the things which God hath prepared for them that love Him. But God hath revealed them unto us by his Spirit"* (1 Cor. 2:9–10). *"Them that love him"*—let us stop right there. Spiritual growth is an issue of love! Everyone who believes on the Lord Jesus Christ is saved, even if they sit in a cold, dead church and the preacher never gives them any knowledge. From my point of view, they have damaged their spiritual growth if they reject knowledge. Believers can fall from grace by leaving grace and going back to law, but they are still saved. I am not going to argue whether people are saved or not saved, as that is foolish on my part, and actually only God knows. If people are ever going on with the Lord, they must have revelation knowledge. As Paul said in the verses above, *"But God hath revealed them unto us by his Spirit."* You can be saved, sit in a church for 50 years, and never receive revelation knowledge; but you will still go to the Father's house. Then, what is the difference between those who don't get revelation knowledge and those who do? It is the love affair.

Some Christians love their church, some love the preacher, some love the doctrine, but they never fall in love with the Christ who is in them. Paul's gospel tells you about the Christ who is in you and how you can fall in love with Christ. These things are revealed to them that love Him. What is the difference between sitting in your home reading this book and going downtown to sit in the big "First Church" in your community? They love God down there, and they are going to hear a good message. They are going to hear a good choir and will feel that they have "been to church" when it is all over. What is the difference? The difference is our love affair!

Revelation knowledge never violates the Word of God. Revelation knowledge brings to you what the Word has always been saying but you could not see because you had on the wrong glasses. The Holy Spirit never violates God's plan. He is always clear, but you have to come to a place where your love for Him is so great that He can trust you with revelation knowledge. You are going to get this knowledge strictly through the Holy Spirit, the revealer of the things of Christ (John 15:26).

A major problem in our spiritual growth is that we don't know how to separate the inner from the outer. The simple fact is that an inner relationship with God is painful because we see that most of what we have done and said in our life is a violation of that knowledge. As you read this book, it may be very painful for you to accept the idea that nothing you have seen, heard, and felt has anything to do with your spiritual growth. You would rather have all the outer things that you have seen, heard, and felt applied as spiritual growth. The outer things are glorious, but they are the difference between the two gospels. They are the difference between Christ in the earthly form and Christ in the believer.

Chapter 11
Review Questions

1. Describe what it usually takes for you to make a change in your belief system.

2. Since you have come to understand the Christ-life message, what identification with your past have you given up as worthless?

3. What are the most important factors that determine your spiritual growth?

4. Explain why the choices you make are important.

5. What does *"until Christ be formed in you"* in Galatians 4:19 mean to you?

6. Explain what is meant by "revelation knowledge."

And when they were escaped, then they knew that the island was called Melita. And the barbarous people shewed us no little kindness: for they kindled a fire, and received us every one, because of the present rain, and because of the cold. And when Paul had gathered a bundle of sticks, and laid them on the fire, there came a viper out of the heat, and fastened on his hand. And when the barbarians saw the venomous beast hang on his hand, they said among themselves, No doubt this man is a murderer, whom, though he hath escaped the sea, yet vengeance suffereth not to live ... but after they had looked a great while, and saw no harm come to him, they changed their minds, and said that he was a god. (Acts 28:1–6)

CHAPTER 12
Paul and Eschatology

Introduction

As we come to the last chapter of this book, I want to deal with the doctrine of eschatology. The word *eschatology* is a theological term meaning the doctrine of end-times. I think you will find this to be a very simple subject to deal with if you rightly divide the Word of Truth. Paul believed and practiced rightly dividing the Word so keenly in his epistles that there is no doubt as to what his feeling was about the end-times.

Most people in Christianity don't know or understand the things of the end-times. The prophecy preachers and book writers of today have mostly ignored Paul's instruction in the Scriptures and his understanding of God's plan for the born-again. Therefore, most believers don't know what is going to happen in the future.

In his teaching on the end-times for the born-again, Paul didn't take one thing out of the book of Daniel. Paul didn't take anything out of the book of Revelation, although he had revelation knowledge. Paul wasn't given any revelation of the end-times except the Rapture of the Church of Jesus Christ. Paul had a clear voice on what will actually happen to the believers who are born again since they are the ones to whom Paul's message is directed.

Bible Division by Prophecy and the Mystery

Paul's message causes us to consider the Scriptures differently, to divide them differently. We have always known there are two parts to the Bible—the Old Testament and the New Testament— but that is not the proper division. Paul effectively divides the Bible by prophecy and mystery. Prophecy includes those parts of God's Word that will happen in the future. It is the largest part of the Scriptures, about four-fifths of the Bible. The subject of prophecy consumes some people because that is really what the majority of the Scriptures are about. Prophecy takes in everything in your Bible with the exception of part of John's gospel, part of John's epistles, part of Peter's epistles, and all of Paul's epistles. These writings comprise the writings of the mystery (Col. 1:27). Therefore, one-fifth of the Bible is given to the mystery and about four-fifths to prophecy.

One-fifth of the Bible deals with this great mystery of how another person lives in the believer and makes the believer acceptable to God. Though there are several mysteries mentioned in the New Testament, this one is the most important. Paul received the revelation of the mystery in the Arabian Desert, and it is clearly defined in Colossians 1:26–27, where it plainly says the mystery is *"Christ in you, the hope of glory."* One-fifth of the Bible deals with this great mystery of how another person lives in the human who believes on Jesus Christ, making him or her acceptable to God.

The first prophecy fulfilled in the Scriptures is in Genesis 3:15, where it states the enmity God put between the serpent's seed and the woman's seed would bruise both the head of the serpent (Satan) and the heel of the woman's seed (Christ, note the reference to the virgin birth). This is the first announcement of Calvary. One of the greatest prophecies in the book of Genesis is Genesis 12:3, where it says one day all the families of this earth will be blessed by Israel, referring to Christ.

I have often been asked why churches have so much trouble. Commingling is the beginning of the problem because it does not give us a firm base in the

Scriptures. You cannot commingle Israel with the Church because they are two different groups of people. What makes them different is that Israel is saved by self-effort. For example, Peter's message on the Day of Pentecost said, *"Repent and be baptized"* (Acts 2:38). To repent and be baptized is something you do. There is a great difference between those who do this and those in Acts 16:31 who were simply told, *"Believe on the Lord Jesus Christ, and thou shalt be saved."* Only as we understand these differences are we able to come to a greater understanding of who and what we are in Christ. Four-fifths of your Bible is written concerning an earthly relationship with God. One-fifth of the Bible deals with a heavenly relationship. The Israelites in the Old Testament are an earthly people who depended on what they themselves did to save themselves—keeping the covenants and obeying God. Everything that happened to them was earthly. All the covenants made to Israel were earthly.

On the other hand, in the mystery, we are an entirely different group of people. We are not of this earth. We are not going to remain on this earth. We are going to be taken off this earth in accordance with the first two chapters of Ephesians, which say at least five times that we are a heavenly people. Our blessings are heavenly, and we are seated in heavenly places with Christ. It is important that you see this. Matthew 25:34 states: *"Then shall the King say unto them on his right hand, Come, ye blessed of my Father, inherit the kingdom prepared for you from the foundation of the world."* The important word you need to circle is *from.* This means the entire gospel of prophecy, the gospel of the kingdom, is *"from the foundation of the world."* Everything God does for earthly people has to do with the earth. From Adam forward, God was in the process of correcting things on this earth. Everything was perfect before Adam and Eve got together at the Tree of the Knowledge of Good and Evil. From that point on, four-fifths of the Bible is a correction of what took place in the Garden of Eden. One day, all the people on earth, who are earthly, are going to see the earth become again like it was with Adam, and even better. The key word *from* is an important point in prophecy. In this verse of Scripture, Jesus is saying to Israel that the kingdom was prepared for them from the foundation of the earth.

The very opposite is stated in Ephesians 1:4, *"According as He has chosen us in him* [Christ] *before the foundation of the world."* The key word here is *before.* You cannot understand prophecy if you don't get these two words straightened out in your mind. Four-fifths of the Bible deals with what God did *from* the foundation of the world. One-fifth deals with what He did *before* the foundation of the world. We who are in Christ, the born-again, are a people who were chosen to be in Christ *before* anything was created. Four-fifths of the Bible deals with what happened from Creation onward and is earthly. It has nothing to do with heavenly things. It had nothing to do with the things God has prepared for the born-again.

Also, these two words constitute the basis for the two gospels, the gospel of circumcision and the gospel of uncircumcision. Paul is very precise in dealing with the subject of the difference between prophecy and the mystery by making a clear distinction between these two gospels. He does not talk about Daniel or the book of Revelation because that material has to do with earthly prophecy. It has nothing to do with heavenly people.

The Apostle Paul deals with two things in his doctrine of the end-times. Paul deals with the Resurrection and the Parousia, which is the Rapture. He does this because we are heavenly people and belong in our Fa-

ther's house. Everywhere I go, Christians are concerned about the end-time and who the antichrist might
be. As a result, these Christians seem to act as if there
is no God, as if they think we have been turned over as
sheep to the wolves. Paul never goes into the end-time
or the antichrist because it is not an important factor
for the born-again.

Prophetic Scriptures for the Born-Again

Two portions of prophetic Scriptures bear out
what is ours in Christ. The first of these is found in 1
Corinthians 15:50–54. Verse 50 says, *"Now this I say,
brethren, that flesh and blood cannot inherit the kingdom of God; neither does corruption inherit
incorruption."* I must say something about this verse
before I go on. The term *"kingdom of God"* is used by
Jesus of Nazareth, who meant one thing, and by the
Apostle Paul who meant another thing. There really
should have been a difference in the translation of this
term. The simple fact is that when Jesus spoke of the
"kingdom of God," He was speaking of the kingdom
of heaven on this earth. He told the disciples to go
preach that the kingdom of heaven on earth was at
hand. When Paul spoke of the kingdom, he spoke of
Christ in us, our hope of glory. The kingdom is now in
us, and Paul said this kingdom of Christ in you cannot
be inherited by flesh and blood. We might ask, *Who
will go into the kingdom of God on this earth?* The answer is *"flesh and blood."* This means many people in
the Millennium, who will be flesh and blood, will participate in the kingdom on earth. You and I may
participate in the Millennium, but we will not be flesh
and blood. We will be spirit beings with bodies like Jesus had when He returned from the grave. Paul is
making a distinction in this verse 50 between those
who are flesh and blood and those who are not. The
flesh and blood people will enter into the kingdom of
God on this earth because flesh and blood cannot enter

the kingdom of God where Christ is life. Neither does corruption inherit incorruption.

First Corinthians 15:51–54 continue:

> *Behold, I show you a mystery; we shall not all sleep* [die]*, but we shall all be changed, In a moment, in the twinkling of an eye, at the last trump: for the trumpet shall sound, and the dead shall be raised incorruptible, and we shall be changed. For this corruptible must put on incorruption, and this mortal must put on immortality. So when this corruptible shall have put on incorruption, and this mortal shall have put on immortality, then shall be brought to pass the saying that is written, Death is swallowed up in victory.*

This is the first portion of Scripture where Paul deals with anything having to do with the end-times of born-again believers. Here he deals with the dead in Christ. I will get to that shortly, but I want you to see here that some of the believers in Corinth, who looked for Jesus to appear in their day, began to worry about what would happen to those who had already died. This portion of Scripture was written to resolve that problem.

Let us now go to the only place where Paul truly dealt with eschatological aspects having to do with born-again believers. In 1 Thessalonians 4:13, he said, *"But I would not have you to be ignorant, brethren, concerning them which are asleep* [or dead]*, that ye sorrow not, even as others which have no hope."* Paul was still concerned with the living believers understanding what will happen to those who have already died. Continuing with verse 14: *"For if we believe that Jesus died and rose again, even so them also which sleep in Jesus will God bring with him."* Circle the two words *in Jesus* because this is your in-Christ message. It is one of the most important prophecy statements for the born-again because it is the only prophecy ever given to the born-again stating that the dead in Christ shall rise.

First Thessalonians 4:15–18 continue,

> *For this we say unto you by the word of the Lord, that we which are alive and remain unto the coming of the Lord shall not prevent them which are asleep* [or are dead]. *For the Lord himself shall descend from heaven with a shout, with the voice of the archangel, and with the trump of God: and the dead in Christ* [this is the second "in Christ" statement] *shall rise first: Then we which are alive and remain shall be caught up together with them in the clouds, to meet the Lord in the air: and so shall we ever be with the Lord. Wherefore comfort one another with these words.*

These are the only two portions of Scripture that deal with eschatology on Paul's part. Neither of these passages has a prior setting or a prior mention. They are two events that belong strictly to the mystery and are spoken of only in the one-fifth of the Bible I defined earlier. They are important because they contain "in Christ" statements.

The Resurrections

Revelation 20:6 states, *"Blessed and holy is he that hath part in the first resurrection: on such the second death hath no power."* The first resurrection has four events to it. The first event is Christ's resurrection. His coming out of the grave was called by Paul the first fruit of resurrection (1 Cor. 15:20, 23), which means there will be more fruit produced as a result of His resurrection. The Scriptures plainly declare that we died in Christ on the cross. We were crucified in Him, buried in Him, resurrected in Him, and we ascended in Him (Rom. 6:4, 6; Eph. 2:4–6; Col. 2:12).

The second event of the first resurrection is the resurrection of believers. We have read statements on this in 1 Corinthians 15 and 1 Thessalonians 4.

The third event of the first resurrection is the resurrection of the Tribulation saints. They don't really have anything to do with us, but it is important to know something about them. The Tribulation saints will probably be people who hear the gospel from Israel and believe, probably those who have not had an opportunity to accept Christ as we have, such as heathen and others who don't know Jesus as we do.

Most Bible-believers understand that people who reject Christ as their Savior in this day of grace go into the Tribulation period, they still will not believe. This is based on the fact that right now they have the Holy Spirit to help them come to Christ, and they will not have the Holy Spirit to help them during the Tribulation period. The only means by which they can know Christ in the Tribulation period will be to suffer greatly. It is hard to believe that people who now have the gospel so freely and easily available will be able to stand against such hard times and accept the gospel.

The fourth event of the first resurrection is the resurrection of the Old Testament saints. I put this before you because I want you to see that all these resurrections are a part of the first resurrection.

The next resurrection takes place at the end of the Millennium and constitutes the second death. There will be no hope for those at the time of the second resurrection. The only hope for people is in Christ's resurrection, but be aware that there are two different aspects of Christ's resurrection. Christ's resurrection and the resurrection of believers in Christ (a part of the first resurrection) all have to do with being in Christ. The other resurrection events will not resurrect people in Christ because they have never been in

Christ. They have never believed on the Lord Jesus Christ and been baptized into His Body. They are a different group of believers.

The Tribulation saints and the Old Testament saints will be resurrected as a part of the first resurrection and go into the Millennium. We have always had an idea that all of God's children are gathered home. That is correct, but we have to watch our terminology. The Old Testament saints are not God's children. They have never been God's children. They will never be God's children because God's plan of grace and the in-Christ message has never been extended to them. They don't belong in the Father's house. When they are resurrected, the Tribulation saints and the Old Testament saints will go directly into the Millennium to rule and reign with Christ on this earth because they are an earthly people. This is the big difference between the earthly and the heavenly people in the Scriptures. Earthly people never go to heaven. The only ones who go to heaven are those who have been baptized into Christ (1 Cor. 12:13). The in-Christ people are the only ones who go to the Father's house because they are the Father's offspring whom He has birthed. The birthing is what separates all people who have ever lived. The birthed people are His own, and they belong with Him. Those who were not birthed by God, who came to salvation through other means, are an earthly people and will remain on this earth. There is no indication in the Scriptures as to what will happen to these earthly people beyond the Millennium. After the time of the Millennium, there will be a new heaven and a new earth (Rev. 21:1).

The division is critical, and you must know the difference between those who are earthly and those who are heavenly. Because of our commingled gospel, many in the Church keep looking at Israel to see what God is doing, but there are no signs that God is dealing with Israel in any way, shape, or form since Acts 28:28. Since the gospel went to the Gentiles, God has had nothing to do with Israel as an earthly people. The moment the Rapture takes place, God's plan will focus again on the earthly people. They will have tribulation, the antichrist, and the Armageddon war. When Jesus comes back to rule and reign on this earth, it will be the beginning of a new Millennium. He does not reign today for those people.

At the present time, God's arms are open to whoever believes (Jew and Gentile), and there is no special offering to Israel. To be saved, Israel must come as the Gentiles do; and once they are saved, they are no longer Jews. The fact that you were a Jew, a Gentile, a German, a Latino, an African-American, or an Irishman makes no difference to God. Once you believe on the Lord Jesus Christ, you are a part of the new-creation race where there is no ethnicity (Gal. 3:28; Col. 3:11).

When you study the topic of resurrection, you will see that only those who have died in Christ go to heaven. Those who did not die in Christ are headed toward the second death. The Tribulation saints will pay a great price to be saved, and they will have a resurrection that takes place when Jesus comes back at the Second Coming.

If you believed on the Lord Jesus Christ, you are a part of the first resurrection. Never doubt or fear what is going to happen to you because you are well provided for. Paul has gloriously covered the point that all corruption will put on incorruption. Mortals will put on immortality (1 Cor. 15:53–54). A glorious change will take place on the resurrection morning for the Church (those born-again) and for those who remain and wait to be caught up to meet Him in the clouds. Right now, you have body pulls that distract you from the Christ who lives in you. It is your body wanting your mind instead of you giving your mind to Christ. On resurrection morning, you will not have body pulls anymore; and for the first time in your existence, your mind will have a clear channel to the Christ who is in you.

The Rapture

This brings up the subject of those who rise up and meet the Lord in the air in what the Scriptures call the "Parousia," which is the Rapture. *"Then we which are alive and remain shall be caught up together with them in the clouds, to meet the Lord in the air"* (1 Thess. 4:17). The Rapture is the catching up of all believers from this earth.

The first important aspect of the Rapture is that Jesus does not come back to this earth for the born-again; we meet Him in the air. That fits because we are a heavenly people. He is not an earthly Christ to us. When He comes back to this earth, He will be King of the world. To us, He is not King; He is Lord and Savior.

We should now look at 1 Thessalonians 4:16, *"For the Lord himself shall descend from heaven with a shout, with the voice of the archangel, and with the trump of God."* This means we no longer look for signs. We listen for sounds. These three sounds—the shout of the Lord, the voice of the archangel, and the trump of God—will not be heard by this world. There will be no forewarning.

On the resurrection morning, we will hear the glorious sound of Jesus shouting because He is coming for us. Nothing that happens in this world signals that Jesus is coming for His own. All the signs you see are for the Second Coming. There are no signs for the Rapture—no warning and no advance knowledge, not one single prophecy to be fulfilled to bring it about.

The Purpose of the Rapture

One purpose of the Rapture is for the Father to receive those He has birthed. Another purpose is to resurrect the dead in Christ. The dead in Christ will come forth victoriously the instant before we are raised up to meet the Lord.

The Rapture is the way we go to the Father's house. I think great numbers of kingdom people don't believe in the Father's house. They believe the Father's house is symbolic because most kingdom preaching is symbolic. They believe the Father's house is our body where Jesus comes to live, which they don't take very seriously anyway. I believe Jesus meant just what He said in John 14:2, *"In my Father's house are many mansions: if it were not so, I would have told you. I go to prepare a place for you."* At the time of Jesus' statement, He was not speaking of something that belonged to the group He was with at that moment. The statement He made was for those who would believe after the Day of Pentecost. Jesus' ministry had crossed over from law to grace just before His death as a bridge to the post-resurrection Dispensation of Grace.

When the Rapture takes place, God's children will all stand before the Father for the first time. What a moment of glory! God is going to look at all the children He has birthed. Christ died on the cross so our Father could have children with His seed and His nature in them. Christ's shed blood accomplished the birthing.

The Rapture will also make the saints whole in body, soul, and spirit. You have never been a whole person. You have always been divided between spirit, soul, and body (1 Cor. 15:37–54; 2 Cor. 1:10; Phil. 3:21). On the resurrection morning, you will become the completed individual God intended you to be.

Spared from the Tribulation Period

The Rapture will also cause those birthed of God to miss the Tribulation period. Most believers in the kingdom message don't believe in the Rapture. They believe the Church will go through the Tribulation. Kingdom preachers on radio and television promote the idea that people need to go through the Tribulation period because the Church is not what it should be. Such preaching does not recognize the fact that believers are individuals, and individual members in the Body of Christ are never dealt with corporately. This faulty idea stems from the belief that man has to come up with something to purify and make the Church holy. It does not recognize that we were purified on the cross!

We were in Christ when He died on the cross. His death is our death. His suffering is our suffering. His hopelessness is our hopelessness. His righteousness is our righteousness. It is all incorporated in Christ. By Christ's death, we are free from the teaching that we must go through the Tribulation. His resurrection is our resurrection.

The people who believe the Church needs to go through the Tribulation period have commingled prophecy and the mystery; and worse still, they don't know what it means to be rebirthed. By not understanding either prophecy or the mystery clearly, they commingle them together to come to a faulty understanding of what is happening to believers.

The fact is that the believer does not need the Tribulation because the wrath of God has already been spent on the cross and we were in Christ on the cross. We say again, His crucifixion is our crucifixion. His death is our death. His Cross is our Cross. These facts need to be established in our mind.

The Rapture vs. the Second Coming

Another Biblical understanding we need to see is the difference between the Rapture and the Second Coming. Sometimes people mean the Rapture (when we meet Jesus in the air) when they say the Second Coming. That is not correct. The Rapture is never the Second Coming because Jesus does not come to earth. The Rapture is for a special group of people who are born again, the Father's offspring. The next time Jesus sets foot on this earth, the earth will come under His command. He will rule and reign as King. He will set foot on Mount Olivet and sit on David's throne in Jerusalem. He will instruct Israel and bring all the nations of this world to Himself. This goes back to the parables, a part of the four-fifths of the Bible that are prophecy. The parables will spring forth and happen just like Jesus of Nazareth said. Everything He gave up when He was on earth the first time will be returned to Him as King. He will be the King of Kings in Jerusalem on His throne. That is the Second Coming, and it has nothing to do with the rebirthed believers. That is not part of our life. That is not part of our history. It is not part of the plan of God for the born-again. We will be in heaven in the Father's house where we belong.

The Rapture removes all believers. To be a part of that heavenly host does not mean you are a good Christian. Also, it does not mean you are very spiritual. It means you have been born again. In the Rapture, God gathers His family together, and those who make the Rapture are the Father's offspring. Many people whom you never thought of as good Christians down here are going to be in the Rapture because they have been born again. You may say, *Well, that means we can live any way we want this side of the Rapture.* Yes, you can, if you want a spanking from your Father (Heb. 12:6–11). You are free to live anyway you choose to live. If you don't love Him enough and do all kinds of mean things, I promise you, He will spank you. Furthermore, you will never put life together.

The Second Coming of Christ is the manifestation of the King. Jesus is not our King. He is King in the kingdom message. He is King to Israel. Pilate put on His cross, *"Jesus of Nazareth the King of the Jews"* (John 19:19). However, He is not the King of the born-again. He is our Savior and our Lord. He is our life, but not our King.

The Church, the Body of Christ, meets the Lord in the air at the Rapture. The Lord sets foot on this earth to establish His earthly kingdom at the Second Coming. These are two different events. At the Rapture, Christ comes for His bride, the Church. At the Second Coming, He returns to deal with Israel. The Rapture is a part of the Dispensation of Grace, and the Second Coming of Jesus begins the final dispensation, the Millennium.

A characteristic of the Rapture is that it is an imminent event, meaning Jesus can come at any time without warning. The early Church believed Jesus could come in their day, which is why Paul wrote about these things. Two thousand years ago, people thought Jesus would come; and we are still looking for Him today. On the other hand, the Second Coming will have innumerable signs preceding it. Jesus was speaking of the Second Coming when He said, *When you see all these things come to pass you will know the end is coming* (Matt 24; Mark 13; Luke 21). Jesus did not introduce the Rapture. He could not speak of it because Paul had not yet received the revelation of Christ in the believer.

The Rapture brings us comfort because we don't belong on earth and we know He is coming for us. In contrast, the Second Coming brings judgment (Matt. 25:31–34). The message of the kingdom is a judgment message. God will punish all the nations that have been against Israel. Once we are raptured and go to be with the Lord, a seven-year period, the Tribulation, will begin (Dan. 9; Matt. 24). During that seven-year period, three important things are going to happen to those of us who have gone to the Father's house.

The first event to happen to us after the Rapture is the Judgment Seat of Christ or the Bema, which is a place of reward (2 Cor. 5:10). God is going to reward those who have been faithful to Him. The Scriptures speak of five different crowns that will be given at that time. The first crown is the incorruptible crown (1 Cor. 9:25). The incorruptible crown is for those who have ruled over their flesh. Keep in mind that you don't rule over your flesh to be saved; you rule over your flesh because you are saved. There is also a crown of rejoicing (1 Thess. 2:19). The crown of rejoicing is for those who present the gospel to the unbeliever. They rejoice whenever someone believes. In James 1:12, a crown of life is mentioned for those who have endured trials. One thing many Christians don't understand is that trials are not a bad thing for believers. Trials are important because our Lord generally gets lovers out of those who have deep trials. Those who suffer quite often have deep love. Most of us know at least someone who has suffered far more in this life than we have. As a result, they really love the Lord. These people seem to have one problem after another, but God is going to reward them with a crown. In 2 Timothy 4:8, a crown of righteousness is mentioned for those who love His appearing. A crown of glory is found in 1 Peter 5:4, for those who feed the flock. This crown is not for preachers alone, but for mothers who raise their children correctly and for people at their work place who constantly feed those around them with truth.

The final events that will happen during the Tribulation will be the Marriage of the Lamb and the Marriage Supper of the Lamb (Rev. 19:7–9). These events involve Christ and His Church. The Church—which was God's plan before the foundation of the world (Eph. 1:4)—has been resurrected and translated and has become the eternal bride of Christ.

While there is much more to learn from Paul, our apostle of grace, I will deal with that in the next book.

Chapter 12
Review Questions

1. Describe what dividing the Bible according to prophecy and the mystery means.

2. What happens in the minds of birthed believers when they read Scriptures about the nation of Israel and apply them to their own lives?

3. Explain the difference between the Rapture and the Second Coming.

4. What happens to the believer at the Judgment Seat of Christ (Bema)?

And when we came to Rome, the centurion delivered the prisoners to the captain of the guard: but Paul was suffered to dwell by himself with a soldier that kept him ... And Paul dwelt two whole years in his own hired house, and received all that came in unto him, preaching the kingdom of God, and teaching those things which concern the Lord Jesus Christ, with all confidence, no man forbidding him. (Acts 28:16–31)

MORE CHRIST-LIFE BOOKS

Christ-life Healing for Body and Soul,
  by Warren Litzman

Jesus Lost in the Church, by Warren Litzman

The Making of a Son, by Warren Litzman

My Notes on the Final Gospel, by Warren Litzman

*The Radical Change in God's Plan at the
  Day of Pentecost,* by Warren Litzman

*Revelation Knowledge and Fourth Dimensional
  Living,* by Warren Litzman

*Rivers of Living Water, Christ-life Daily Devotions
  and Commentaries,* by Beryl Woledge

*This Then Is the Message Which We Have Heard of
  Him,* by Warren Litzman

The Unashamed Christian, by Warren Litzman

MORE CHRIST-LIFE BOOKLETS

The Birthing, by Warren Litzman

Christ Liveth in Me, by Warren Litzman

This Same Jesus Is Coming Back Again,
  by Warren Litzman

To Whom Little Is Forgiven, the Same Loveth Little,
  by Warren Litzman

Why Don't Churches Preach the Revelation of Jesus Christ? by Warren Litzman

Why It Makes Good Sense to Be a Christ-life Believer, by Warren Litzman

Why Blood? by Warren Litzman

Learn more at www.christ-life.org.